GRANTING JOY: AN EMPLOYEE ENGAGEMENT ROADMAP

GRANTING JOY: AN EMPLOYEE ENGAGEMENT ROADMAP

Published by Joy Grant

Granting Joy: An employee engagement roadmap

By

Joy Grant

@ Joy Grant

Cataloguing for Information Publication
Published by Joy Grant
ETOBICOKE, Ontario, Canada
ISBN: 9781084124769
@ 2020, Joy Grant

Dedication Page

To Dr. Joseph and Mrs. Agnes Grant, my parents

Granting Joy: An employee engagement roadmap
Table of Contents

Introduction—p. 7
Chapter 1—p. 16
Chapter 2—p. 36
Chapter 3—p. 51
Chapter 4—p. 72
Chapter 5—p. 89
Chapter 6—p. 101
Chapter 7—p. 113
Chapter 8—p. 127
Conclusion—p.139
Acknowledgments—p. 141
About the Author—p. 142

Introduction: Granting Joy: An employee engagement roadmap

Practice what you preach! For 20+years, I have been practicing and now it's time to share what has worked for me in the various Fortune 500 companies where I have been successfully employed, delivering results and engaging cross-functional teams to achieve those audacious corporate and personal goals.

I have always been a proponent of engaging employees to drive business results. Even as a young engineer, I believed in the power of people and their desire to do their best to solve complex problems, execute major projects, and unearth ground-breaking ideas from within.

This book outlines a simple roadmap that is from a practitioner's point of view. And, it is buoyed by the current research that supports the roadmap and its methods. My objective is to compel other managers, business leaders, and teachers to get on the employee engagement bus by providing a practical roadmap that yields results.

Joy Grant, P.Eng., MBA, LSSBB, has 20+ years of experience at various Fortune 500 companies across manufacturing industries from plastics to pharma to food. Her first job in quality test engineering allowed her to develop her leadership style collaborating with and coaching students and new graduates. Throughout her career, Joy has traveled on work assignments to Turkey, Kyrgyzstan, France, throughout Canada and the USA engaging with teams to implement, execute, and continuously improve processes, programs, and products. As a team leader, Joy builds on and leverages her team member's enthusiasm and grants her employees ownership of their tasks and goals so they could be leaders of their work. She believes that the vast majority of employees want to succeed and do a good job so Joy focuses on people, results, and Continuous Improvement tools to achieve personal and corporate goals, attaining overall business success for her employers.

Chapter by Chapter Brief Summary:

With Chapter 1, the goal is to demonstrate the powerful synergy that can be created in the workplace when three key concepts drive an organisation's culture and cohesiveness.

These three key concepts are *discretionary effort*, *employee engagement*, and *internal communications*, and together they make an explosive combination that will catapult your department toward success. I will show you how effective internal communications can drive employee engagement and lead to an overall higher level of discretionary effort in the workplace.

With Chapter 2, employee engagement starts with *leadership*. The adage "charity begins at home" applies also to the workplace to help us recognise that leadership begins at the level at which managers come into direct contact with their employees.

Employee engagement begins, therefore, not with the leadership of a vice-president (VP) or the Human Resources department, but right there in the office with the direct line manager who faces the team on a day-to-day basis. It is this particular manager who represents the company's closest connection to the employees whose daily involvement and enthusiasm require fostering. Because this direct connection is crucial, so is the leader that can make this connection and develop a relationship with the important front-line employees at that level of production.

Chapter 3 introduces a topic that has always been one of my favourites: **employee appreciation**. The American Heritage dictionary defines appreciation as the "thankful recognition" of another based on the actions they have performed. This definition includes not only **gratitude** but a **public demonstration** of gratitude that leads to the recognition of this act of service not just by the recognizer (you) but by others who are also involved in achieving the organisation's common goal.

With Chapter 4, it is noted that teamwork and collaboration are becoming more and more necessary in today's workplace. Trust, respect, autonomy, ownership, and a problem-solving mindset all help to allow a team to achieve its goals. And, an empowering leadership style allows a leader to share power and cultivate an environment of engagement.

Chapter 5 conveys that communication is an important aspect of business strategy, whether it's for sharing the vision, tactics, and directives or for building internal cohesion. Here, we will see the benefits of various communication avenues and how these can get the attention of your employees; including communicating to employees from certain generations as their communication preferences differ. In Chapter 6, we discuss getting your employees involved in the operation by seeking their opinions, ideas, and solutions. And, as an empowering leader, allow your employees to develop these ideas and even be part of the process to see these ideas become reality. This allows for growth and deeper understanding that supports continued engagement.

With Chapter 7, the use of Lean tools in the workplace can give a business a competitive advantage - driving down costs and increasing profits. Linking lean tools to lean management ideas can leverage employee's strengths, putting them to use, and getting the best out of your employee resources.

With Chapter 8, an important aspect of cementing a company's relationship to its employees lies in how effectively it celebrates its successes and how well it constructs an ongoing mechanism for employee rejuvenation. Note that celebrations do not have to be elaborate or expensive; even a tiny show of gratitude or a public acknowledgment can count as a celebratory gesture and motivate or reinvigorate the employees that receive it.

The conclusion summarizes the book though a schematic of the roadmap that you can post in your office and use in your everyday journey to lead and engage your employees to future successes.

Chapter 1: Engagement

Summary: Three concepts *discretionary effort*, *employee engagement*, and *internal communications* can help to improve any company. This chapter will discuss these three concepts in more detail. My goal for this chapter is to demonstrate the powerful synergy that can be created in the workplace when these three concepts come together to drive an organisation's culture.

Together, these three concepts make an explosive combination that will catapult your business toward success. Throughout this book, I will outline a roadmap which is my *common-sense driven plan* for enabling communications and a leadership style that can build an engaged workforce.

Discretionary Effort

Discretionary effort describes the kind of surplus energy existing within an employee even after s/he has done the required work and has been rewarded for it. This surplus energy is latent—it is there and even available for input into the organisation, but will only be unleashed if that employee is *willing* to make the effort to do so. Aubrey Daniels (2019) puts it simply: beyond the minimum level of work required, "discretionary effort is the level of effort people could give *if they wanted to*" (par. 1; emphasis added). What can be understood from these definitions is that employee willingness is important to extracting discretionary effort. While this certainly depends to some extent on a team leader's ability to identify potential, the issue of willingness becomes relevant when we realize that only the employee knows *how much* untapped potential lies within him/her. The obvious question is, then, how can an employee like this be made willing to take advantage of their full potential? We'll get to this soon.

Employee Engagement

Research by William H. Macey (Valtera Corporation) and Benjamin Schneider (2008) with the University of Maryland shows that managers and researchers consider employee engagement a "desirable condition [that] has an organisational purpose and connotes involvement, commitment, passion, enthusiasm, focused effort, and energy" (4). What these experts are referring to is a managerial approach that creates ideal conditions in which all members of the team feel motivated to perform to their highest levels while on the job (MacLeod and Clark, 2015, 8). At this point, the connection between employee engagement and the willingness to do more than the minimum starts becoming apparent. This is especially true since engagement creates conditions in which employees are motivated to expend discretionary effort in the organisation.

Internal Communication: Internal communication mechanisms include emails, memos, and corporate networks on social media. It involves any method individuals or groups within the organisation can use to communicate ideas between or among its other members. Internal Communications is vital to the health of an organisation. The Coca-Cola Company and Bayer Corporation consider internal communication to be of such great importance that each has developed its tool to measure it and to gain feedback from employees on how effectively the company communicates with them (Ilif, 12 August 2016, par. 3-4). Yet, while the technical definition of internal communications involves information sharing within the organisation to support business practices, I would also like to extend it to the kind of communication that involves open, honest, and mutual information sharing among executives, managers, and employees. The difference I want to highlight is that with this measure of communication, top-level executives can show that they consider lower-level employees an integral part of the team.

Because of this, my broader definition works in an organisational culture that includes even lower-level employees in the company's decisions so that they too feel like the stakeholders that I believe they are.

Before I elaborate on the roadmap, let's get some more information about why communication within an organisation is critical to its success. Not just in its public role as a player on the competitive market, but also internally where the organisation exists as a social and cooperative space for employees to interact.

Senior director of marketing and author of *The Excellence Habit* by Vlad Zachary (2015) explains that open, candid, and transparent communications put everyone in a place of mutual understanding. "We have certainly heard before that employees are an organisation's most prized assets," Anne M. Mulcahy. Employers make statements like that all the time, but the question remains whether their behaviours show that they believe in these statements. I would like to help leaders and managers act like they believe that employees are their key stakeholders, and internal communications is a key starting point in achieving this. Companies are now beginning to see the value of Internal Communications—and this has certainly not always been the case.

- Coca-Cola's Ambassador programme has launched a tool for measuring communication *within* the organisation that has benefits for consumers outside the company and, as a result, improves the image of the brand (Ilif par. 3; Service Design at Coca-Cola GBS).

- Western Sydney University has dedicated an arm of its resources to put into place tools and strategies that transfer executive ideas down to the level of staff and students. The administrators recognize the importance of utilizing these tools as executive-level administrators, but also the importance of making them available for smaller projects being implemented at the student level. This ensures that each department of the university uses "the best channels to communicate a message" (WSU par. 2).

"These examples show that communication has evolved from an old model of a mere Human Resource function for sharing basic information with employees to one where employees have become exposed even to corporate strategy and business goals" Keith Burton.

Organisations run on many wheels. The fluid rotation of these wheels relies on the unimpeded circulation of a variety of types of information.

- ***The general and particular objectives of the business***: these include the company's overall mission as well as the rationale behind the day-to-day tactics that are implemented and which employees are expected to carry out.
- ***Organisational performance***: this involves the overall effectiveness of the general and particular objectives. The extent to which these goals are being met (that is, whether the company is experiencing high, medium, or low performance) has an impact on the overall health of the organisation
- ***Potential roadblocks to success***: this involves the knowledge of impediments to look out for and to avoid to keep performance high and the organisation on track toward its objectives.
- ***Individual employee feedback***: this lets management know when or why performance might be compromised, roadblocks might be ahead, and why goals might not be met

When employers openly share information like this with employees, they create an open environment that fosters a sense of belonging. Furthermore, this leads employees to feel a sort of ownership of the organisation, especially if they come to believe in its continued success and that they have a stake in it. As Chad Brooks (June 11, 2015) recognizes, "effective communication with employees results in workers who both rate their employers' reputations favorably and feel their company's best years are still to come" (par. 2). This causes them to become more engaged. In my experience, most employees want the organisations that they work for to succeed and are eager to contribute to making this happen. Sharing information provides employees with the tools needed to contribute substantially and constructively. Because Internal Communications allows the employee to understand the needs of the business, it gives them a chance to finds ways of meeting those needs. In other words, this allows employees to get creative to solve problems and/or continually improve the company's operation. It allows the employee to see beyond their limited role in the company and to develop a big picture mindset.

Investing in Employees
"More than half of employees surveyed reported that communication and honesty are key factors that drive their engagement on their jobs" (Tavakoli, 2015).

In his report on a study performed in 2015 by MSW ARS Research, Mahan Tavakoli carefully points out that given the importance of the employee to the organisation, managers would miss out if they did not invest in each member of the team. As Dale Carnegie Training's Regional Vice President and Chief Diversity Officer, Tavakoli has had enough experience with managing workforces to understand that an engaged employee "represents [a company's] most significant investment and ultimately determines the success or failure of the organisation" (par. 1). Because of this, rewards in the form of money, benefits, and even flexibility in determining work hours are not enough to get the best from employees. Over and above these is the employee's need to feel part of a team, to feel appreciated, and to engage in the goals of the organisation. More than money, it is trust and *communication* that drives this engagement. Employees want to be trusted with the relevant information so that they understand what the organisation's goals are and can make them their own. Then, once their goals are aligned with the organisation's objectives, employees can assess their abilities to see what they can bring to the table.

In fact, according to the *American Psychology Association Harrison Interactive Workplace Survey* carried out as part of their Psychologically Healthy Workplace Program, "employees who report feeling valued by their employers are more likely to report they are motivated to do their very best for their employer" (Workplace Survey, March 2012, p. 5). Particularly, the researchers report that this increase in motivation—which leads to the discretionary effort—occurs in sixty percent of employees whose employers make the effort to keep them in the know and to make them feel valued as a result.

The likelihood of encouraging discretionary effort in employees links Internal Communications and employee engagement a vital one for leaders to cultivate. Throughout this book, we will review how business performance can be improved by leveraging employee engagement. Here is the outline of the roadmap — it is my common sense driven plan for enabling Internal Communications and a leadership style that can result in discretionary effort on the employee's part and lead toward an engaged workforce.

The roadmap: A common-sense-driven plan

- **Leadership**

Leadership does not start with the protocols and tenets of an HR department; rather leadership should begin with the employee's relationship to his/her ***direct supervisor***. As a team leader, you are the company's most direct connection to its employees, and retention, as well as productivity, depends on how well you can communicate the company's objectives and rally the employees' support. Success in this area leads to a culture of employee engagement within the company, and every team leader should strive to have an engaged-employee culture because employees are the most valuable assets in an organisation. Because of this, even though leaders are often busy with the many other responsibilities of their job, they must still find or *make* the time to connect with employees. And, because a little effort in employee appreciation can go a long way, leaders should be kind, compassionate, and caring toward these persons who rely on their guidance and encouragement to do the work that is so vital to the company.

- **Getting employees involved/Lean Tools**

Lean philosophy involves using efficient means of creating more value for the employee (Lean). It brings a benefit to the workplace, as it can make employees' jobs easier by giving them greater knowledge about the company's goals and a clearer view of their steps needed to reach them. Employees should have:

- A focused list of steps or a methodology to follow when approaching problems
- Employees should not only be well trained but also provided with consistent coaching to help them continually improve their skill sets
- Employees should be given the time and space they need to work on these problems (Norval, June 26, 2014).

A manager's use of lean tools reduces the uncertainty or ambiguity of the various tasks employees must handle, and this in turn gives them more control over the environment they work in. Involving and especially *challenging* your employees to use lean tools to solve problems, has the effect of enhancing the value chain and the final customer experience. And, it drives engagement! Because of these benefits, leaders should educate employees on the value of these lean tools so that they will be more enthusiastic about using them. Furthermore, lean tools help solve problems that might hamper employee productivity — successful usage of lean tools can help relieve stresses thereby creating an environment that translates into greater ease in handling your job as a leader.

- **Frequent open & honest communications**

Communication is critical to employee engagement and must be a *two-way street*. A leader must strive to maintain open and honest communications that use all the various verbal and non-verbal ways people communicate. Using a variety of communication methods helps to reach a wide variety of people who will very likely have different preferred communication styles. These range from one-on-one meetings to social media. In short, a good manager *leaves her office* and gets to where the work happens to spend quality time in the presence of her employees. This makes her accessible and employees more likely to reach out to her if there is a problem.

- **Celebrating success**

Successful companies celebrate their successes with the employees that helped them to reach that level. It is important to note that team leaders should *celebrate* success and not merely always *reward* success. I think many would agree that there is a difference. Giving employees monetary compensation doesn't always make them go the extra mile, whereas simple gestures like a high five, a thank-you, a heartfelt e-mail, even a public announcement celebrate success in a way that encourages other employees to behave in similar beneficial ways. Remember, however, that leaders need to be true to their environment, values, employee culture, *but also their budgets*! Bonuses are nice, but the budget doesn't always allow it, and since money doesn't *always* motivate employees, it makes sense to look into equally effective ways of securing employees' enthusiastic input.

Celebrating success gives the desired positive reinforcement; it encourages employees not only to repeat the behaviours that led to that success but also to come up with innovative ways of exceeding them. Such celebrations can be done on an individual, team, or corporate levels. For this reason, team building activities are also rewards, and they enhance the collaborative abilities of a group. Having team lunches, for example, will encourage budding solidarity within an entire department, whereas bonuses (while good) will likely reward employees only at the individual level. In the final analysis, however you choose to celebrate success, do remember: ***positive reinforcement begets the desired behaviours***.

This is my common-sense-driven roadmap for engaging employees. But how did this come to be? This personal-common-sense-this-is-what-worked-for-me approach is a product of more than two decades of experience working in healthy and unhealthy work environments. It reflects my training both in and out of school, but especially on-the-job experience observing and learning from good and not-so-good leaders. As Gerard Seijts (2014) says in *Good Leaders Learn*, "leaders can potentially learn from their every experience and from any leader they've seen in action—good or bad" (18). In my years of being an employee who was sometimes valued and sometimes not, I have had time to reflect not only on my changing behaviours in these different work environments but also those of my colleagues who experienced the same organisational culture. Again, Seijts supports this kind of open-minded learning, stating that "leaders can learn from their peers, the people who report to them, competitors, partners, and suppliers. And they can learn from their critics" (18). Later, when I became a team leader, I took these experiences with me. It is through personal reflection, a willingness to learn from everyone, and years of honing my leadership style, that I have come to understand that employees are *eager to build something they know they are a part of*. Therefore, open and honest communication is key in motivating employees to work harder and to feel that their efforts are worthwhile.

I will now share with you some of the skills I gained during these experiences that helped to shape the roadmap:

1. **Trust**

A necessary skill for any leader is the ability to inspire trust in her employees. As stakeholders, employees need to know that they can believe in what you say and confidently follow your lead. As Ray Silverstein (January 22, 2010) notes in *Entrepreneur*'s series on leadership, "people are not willing to recognize someone as their leader unless they trust them, not just intellectually, but ethically and morally as well" (para. 3). Needless to say, if your employees don't trust you, they will not give you the results that you want. And naturally, you must do what is necessary to earn this trust. As a leader, you must be honest, consistent, credible, competent, and committed. When you've exhibited all these qualities to your employees, then their belief in and support of you will grow (Gupta, Modgil & Gunasekaran, 2020).

And of course, trust works both ways. As a leader, it is imperative that you also extend trust wisely to your stakeholders. Former U.S. secretary of state Henry Stimson recognized that persons return trust or distrust to anyone who first shows those behaviours toward them (Covey and Merrill, 2006, 249). Naturally, you will need to be wise when extending your trust, but doing this inspires your team not only to trust you but also to trust each other. An environment of trust—where people can count on every member of the team to make their contributions toward a common goal—is the very definition of an organisation in which employees are engaged and performing to their highest capabilities. As Stephen Covey and Rebecca Merrill (2006) say, taking the time to build trust between you and your team members produces results.

2. **Communication**

Before your team can solve a problem or reach a goal, each member must have a full understanding of what is at stake. Ray Silverstein (January 22, 2010) addresses this issue when he says, "people won't follow someone unless they're convinced that person knows where they're going" (par. 3). To have a vision is to know where you're going, and to communicate that vision is to let others understand that you know where you're going so that they can make an informed decision about whether or not to come along. The University of Kansas's Work Group for Community Development (WGCD) (2018), states that the ability of the leader to communicate a vision is an important component of team motivation. The importance of having a vision is that as a leader you can use it "to lead—to mobilize and inspire people so that others want to join you in making your vision a reality" (WGCD) (2018). Many other articles and books cover the important aspects of communicating a vision, so I digress. In my experience, what has been critical in beginning to engage others has been a commitment to asking open-ended questions that get your employee talking and collaborating. Hand in hand with questioning is listening (Gupta, Modgil & Gunasekaran, 2020). Listening will foster the sharing of information and development of ideas, which can then lead to a more innovative and productive work environment. *Forbes* contributor Mike Myatt (February 9, 2010) has astutely observed, "While some may be impressed with how well you speak, the right people will be impressed with how well you listen" (par. 1). When you take the time to ask questions and then listen *attentively* to the response, your stakeholders feel valued, appreciated, and supported (Henrique & Godinho Filho, 2020). More importantly, they feel they are in a safe environment that will support their ideas—and the sharing of these innovative ideas represents precisely the discretionary effort you want your employees to make. I have seen this open communicative atmosphere lead to increasing employees' interest in the work itself, which has in turn increased performance and engagement.

3. **Developing Others**

I want people to succeed and to be their best. This has quite naturally prompted me to help others improve their productivity and their lives. Unfortunately, however, for some leaders, this skill is not well understood or even easy to practice. Glen Llopis's (February 2, 2015) article in *Forbes* says that "the best leaders know how to get the most out of people" (par. 1). This is meant not in a mercenary way of taking without giving, but in a way that means the leader invests in those people and pushes them toward reaching their fullest potential. There are countless benefits when a leader enables the full potential of others. Investing in the careers of subordinates is beneficial to the leader: when employees' careers flourish, it means their productivity is on the rise, and increased productivity adds value to the organisation as a whole (Henrique & Godinho Filho, 2020).

Related to the desire for success in others is the skill of delegating for development. Each member of the organisation has his or her special skill, and as Llopis's (February 2, 2015) article also assures us, "The best leaders are those that can identify and appreciate the differences [each employee] brings to the table and knows how to put them to full use" (par. 5). When the various skills of team members complement each other, their leader must understand the role each member plays to correctly delegate responsibility. Not only will this help to boost efficiency, but it will also enhance the growth and development of the delegates' capabilities. Ultimately, all this leads to the benefit of the organisation and the team. Finally, developing others and delegating responsibility to your team shows them that they are trusted, valued, and competent. Therefore, when you develop your team and get a win, it's also important to celebrate that success. All of this is an aid to employee engagement.

So, do you remember that "obvious question" we asked much earlier in the chapter: how can employees be made willing to expend the discretionary effort? All the things we have been discussing so far combine to answer this question. By communicating with employees, motivating them to reach their potential, and converting them into engaged employees who understand your vision and how they are a part of it, you create the perfect conditions in which employees become willing to give their best for the team.

Definitions

Discretionary effort: doing more than expected; going above and beyond the minimum.

Employee engagement: The extent to which employees feel passionate about their jobs are committed to the organisation, and put discretionary effort into their work.

Internal communications (IC): The sharing of information within an organisation for business purposes.

References

Brooks, Chad. (June 11, 2015). "Communication is Key to Genuine Employee Engagement." *Business News Daily.* http://www.businessnewsdaily.com/8095-effective-employee-communication.html

"Coca-Cola Ambassador Program." (2016). Service Design at Coca-Cola GBS. https://vimeo.com/132725738

Covey, Stephen, and Rebecca Merrill. (2006). *The Speed of Trust.* Free Press.

Daniels, Aubrey. (2019). "Discretionary Effort." Aubrey Daniels International. http://aubreydaniels.com/discretionary-effort

"Developing and Communicating a Vision." (2018). *Community ToolBox. The* University of Kansas.

http://ctb.ku.edu/en/table-of-contents/leadership/leadership-functions/develop-and-communicate-vision/main

Gupta, S., Modgil, S., & Gunasekaran, A. (2020). Big data in lean six sigma: a review and further research directions. *International Journal of Production Research*, *58*(3), 947-969.

Henrique, D. B., & Godinho Filho, M. (2020). A systematic literature review of empirical research in Lean and Six Sigma in healthcare. *Total Quality Management & Business Excellence*, *31*(3-4), 429-449.

Iliff, Rebekah. (12 August 2016). "Best Practices for Effective Internal Communications." *Forbes*. https://www.forbes.com/sites/forbesagencycouncil/2016/08/12/best-practices-for-effective-internal-communications/#522fefef7292

Lean Enterprise Institute. (2019). "What is Lean?" https://www.lean.org/WhatsLean/

Macey, William H., and Benjamin Schneider. (2008). "The Meaning of Employee Engagement." *Industrial and Organisational Psychology.* Vol. 1. pp. 3-30.

MacLeod, David, and Nita Clarke. (2015). *Engaging for Success: Enhancing Performance through Employee Engagement.* http://engageforsuccess.org/wp-content/uploads/2015/08/file52215.pdf

Myatt, Mike. (9 February 2010). "Why Most Leaders Need to Shut Up and Listen." *Forbes.* https://www.forbes.com/sites/mikemyatt/2012/02/09/why-most-leaders-need-to-shut-up-listen/#73f666356ef9

Norval, Al. (June 26, 2014). "Back to Basics – Employee Engagement." *Lean Pathways.* http://blog.leansystems.org/2014/06/back-to-basics-employee-engagement.html

Seijts, Gerard. (2014). *Good Leaders Learn: Lessons from Lifetimes of Leadership.* Routledge...

Silverstein, Ray. (January 22, 2010). "Great Leaders Inspire Trust: If People Don't Trust You to Follow through, They Simply Won't Follow." *Entrepreneur.* https://www.entrepreneur.com/article/204816

Tavakoli, Mahan. (February 3, 2015). "Honesty and Communication Drive Employee Engagement." (Dale Carnegie Training). *TrainingMag.com.* https://trainingmag.com/honesty-and-communication-drive-employee-engagement

"Workplace Survey." (March 2012). *American Psychological Association.* Harris Interactive. Psychologically Healthy Workplace Program. https://www.apa.org/news/press/releases/phwa/workplace-survey.pdf

WSU. (2019). "Internal Communication." *Internal Communication Department.*

https://www.westernsydney.edu.au/internalcomms

Zachary, V. (2015). *The Excellence Habit – How Small Changes In Our Mindset Can Make A Big Difference In Our Lives: For All Who Feel Stuck*. United States: Central Street Publications.

Chapter 2: Leadership

Summary: This chapter develops the concept of *employee engagement* further. Establishing a relationship between employees and their *front-line managers* and *direct supervisors* is important for *building connections* and *bringing out the best in a company's employees*.

Employee engagement starts with *leadership*. The adage "charity begins at home" applies also to the workplace to help us recognise that leadership begins at the level at which managers come into direct contact with their employees (Belhadi, Kamble, Zkik, Cherrafi & Touriki, 2020).

Employee engagement begins, therefore, not with the leadership of a vice-president (VP) or the Human Resources department, but right there in the department with the direct line manager who faces the team on a day-to-day basis. It is this particular manager who represents the company's closest connection to the employees whose daily involvement and enthusiasm require fostering. Because this direct connection is crucial, so is the leader that can make this connection and develop a relationship with the important line-employees at that level of production (Belhadi, Kamble, Zkik, Cherrafi & Touriki, 2020).

Employees want to hear messages about engagement from the person they report to, not only from a distant leader like a senior manager or VP. They may often consider such high-level executives to be less knowledgeable about the day-to-day difficulties of the work they as employees perform and may even resent their input. In contrast to this, employees view their direct manager or supervisor as someone who can provide concrete suggestions and directions in important matters related to the details of their work. They view direct managers, therefore, as persons worthy of soliciting and fostering their engagement. In the Harvard Business Review article "Let First-Level Supervisors Do their Job," W. Earl Sasser, Jr. and Frank S. Leonard (March 1980) identify a need to create a balance between the roles played by managers at different levels. They recognize that "First-level supervisors must be able to harmonize the demands of management, the demands of the collective workforce [...], and the demands of the workers with the requirements for doing the tasks at hand" (par. 1). The job of translating these demands is a very important one, and it grants the manager a significant amount of influence in the organisation.

One vice president has noted that such managers "can probably have more influence on our productivity, worker absenteeism, product quality, the morale of our workforce, labor relations, and cost reduction than any other group in the company" (Sasser, Jr. and Leonard, March 1980, par. 2). These factors listed here are all related to employee engagement, and direct managers have a large hand in infusing it into the organisation's culture (Kaswan & Rathi, 2020).

Employees rely on **direct managers** not only for the creation of an organisational culture but also for clues on how the engagement culture is evolving—even if they might not express their desires in exactly those words or understand it in those terms. For this reason, a leader has to lead by example. Sasser, Jr., and Leonard recognize that one of the roots of the term "supervisor" is a lead person whose example is followed by the group. They write, "the lead man served as an example for other work-crew members. He often set the pace by calling out a cadence to synchronize the crew's physical movements. The lead man was part of the actual work, and yet he was responsible for the behavior of the whole group" (March 1980, par. 19).

A supervisor's inclusion in the group at this level requires walking in the shoes of the employee, being there for them when they need support and advice every day, and acting the part of a leader that cares about their welfare and growth. It means not simply knowing their everyday tasks and how their jobs should be performed, but also knowing them as people—knowing how to get the best out of them. Only a direct supervisor can do that. This means as a direct manager, everyone in the department watches you and your actions, so your voice and your ability to relate to employees sets the tone for the organization (Kaswan & Rathi, 2020).

At this point in the discussion, it makes sense to note that successful employee engagement is not a program to be implemented. Rather, it is a culture that needs to be adopted. This should give you a clue as to the important investment that must be made by you as a manager into the relationship you have with your employees—because organisational cultures are not created overnight. Consequently, any change you want to make to the culture also will not be implemented instantaneously and will require the trust of your employees to stick with the plan and see it through. This means you want to do it right the first time to engage employees quickly and securely, because not only does the organisation depend on their engagement, but the employees themselves appreciate it (Kaswan & Rathi, 2020). Note the enormous benefit that the following variables directly related to employee engagement have on employees, as recorded in this study by Dow Scott of Loyola University and Tom McCullen of Hay Group (June 2010).

"The impact of intangible rewards on employee engagement is perceived as very high with the work environment or organisation climate rated at sixty-one percent; work-life balance rated at fifty-five percent; the nature of the job or quality of work rated at sixty-nine percent; and career development opportunities rated at fifty-nine percent" (June 2010, p. 7).

What this shows is that employees consider opportunities to become engaged in their work environment to be rewarded for their jobs! So, engagement must be pursued quickly and unwaveringly.

But timing is everything. The rate at which organisational culture can be cultivated depends rather heavily on a variety of aspects of the organisation and its people. To measure the levels of engagement, Edmans (March 24, 2016) gauged satisfaction using several variables—"respect, fairness, pride, and camaraderie"—all of which will need to work together to advance what we have defined as an organisational culture of employee engagement (Edmans, March 24, 2016, par. 3). Yet, despite the sheer number of factors that a leader must consider when developing a culture of engaged employees, do note that it is possible to execute a clear plan of action! Making the effort to start creating a culture of employee engagement early in the life of the department will be a worthwhile investment.

But, you might ask, what's so great about a culture of employee engagement? Why even bother with it? Well, research shows that organisations that have a noticeable culture of engagement significantly outperform those without key metrics such as profitability, productivity, and customer ratings. Allen (2014) refers to research that has shown not just how profitable culture of employee engagement is, but also how detrimental its opposite, disengagement, really is to a company's bottom line. And what I mean is, this translates to a benefit in dollar amounts that the implementation of an across-the-board engagement culture would bring. Not only would this "result in a significant increase in productivity per employee" but it would "amount to between £52 billion and £70 billion in productivity gains nationwide [UK] per year" (Allen, 2014, 2).

Another example of research that supports this very significant monetary result is a longitudinal study done by London Business School finance professor Alex Edmans (March 24, 2016). This study demonstrates that the culture of engagement that comes from investment in satisfied employees has contributed to consistently higher stock market performance. And this is true for not just a few companies for a short period but for the 100 highest-profile U.S. companies over 28 years (Edmans, March 24, 2016). Edman's research findings fly in the face of the "conventional wisdom" that resources spent on employees equate to resources (i.e. profits) being taken away from shareholders and stakeholders. In reality, Edmans has found that a leader who chooses "not to invest in employee morale" and therefore in the workplace's engagement culture—will very likely "hurt the company's long-term performance" (par. 10). The bottom line is that the benefits of sacrifices made to create a culture of employee engagement significantly and measurably "outweigh the costs" (par. 7).

Engaged employees exhibit passion and energy for their work. They go beyond being merely satisfied with their job to being highly motivated and involved, caring deeply about the business and its success. Their demonstrated enthusiasm, creativity, and care also result in reduced accidents, reduced turnover, and even reduced absenteeism—all translating into dollars earned or saved for the organisation. An engagement culture such as that which produces this result requires time and continuous effort. As Melanie Allen (2014) says, "an effective change programme delivers not just a mindset shift; it also delivers a plan and process for behavioural change to enable sustainable results" (3). And it begins with the engagement of the leaders themselves because how a leader feels about the organisation will affect how they lead; their dedication (or lack) will rub off on their employees.

Yet leaders are often much too busy to address these aspects of culture that will drive employee engagement. But they must find the time because as a leader, your employees are your only assets and you need to be good to them: challenge them, celebrate them, even love them! Perhaps the best reason of all for adopting a culture of engagement is that it makes your job as a leader easier! Recognise their efforts; celebrate their successes; comment privately or publicly on their achievement. This sends a strong message of gratitude not just to the individuals, but also to the teams of people that get the job done. For not only does this promote the cohesion of the team, but it just plain makes the employees happy. And as we all know, happy employees are more productive, and the reason for that is the increased levels of engagement such a person feels about their workplace. Beyond these gains—which are indeed significant—the manager can have the assurance that the euphoria which inevitably comes with celebrating each success can carry the team through until the next achievement.

I realise that the ideal organisational situation described above can be difficult to achieve, so here are a few things you can do to encourage your employees' engagement.

1. **Build connections**

It is OK to be friendly—it's the twenty-first century! By now we know that leadership is all about relationships, and despite the old saying "familiarity breeds contempt," it's also true that distant snobbishness does not foster strong feelings of camaraderie and loyalty in any business relationship. Successful leaders are empathic: they learn to understand the situations of their employees and they put people first. Talk to your employees and ask about their weekend, their pets, their kids. And share your stories too! Employees are people, and people are social beings. They lead full lives in those times when you're not overseeing them, so ask questions about those lives and remember the answers. Even follow-up!

One report published by the Harvard Business Review Analytic Service (HBRAS, 2013) shows that employers prioritize employee engagement by identifying employees' "specific aspects of feelings/emotions about working there" (HBRAS, 2013, p. 10). Those are pretty personal questions. So don't expect to get honest answers to questions like those if you've never tried to get to know these employees on a personal level. As leaders, we are constantly trying to move people in the direction of our vision, which involves the corporation's goals. This is important, but we can do this faster, easier, and more enjoyable if we have a strong connection with our employees. Learn about them. Old school hierarchies and top-down leadership styles are not necessarily considered best practice in the twenty-first century.

2. **Walk Around**

An entire philosophy has developed around the concept of management by walking around (MBWA). Just do a simple Google search and you will find several hits. I have my take on this philosophy, and it's to emphasize how MBWA allows you as a leader to reach out and be present with your employees—your operation. To begin with, a manager who's on her feet and touching base with the employees just plain looks engaged. From the get-go! Beyond mere appearances, though, walking around also gives you a chance to visit employees one on one, and gives them a chance to feel special because you're visiting them on their turf and granting them an opportunity to be heard. They can share issues with you, questions, concerns—and maybe even provide a viable solution to a nagging business problem by granting you a novel perspective on it. Overall, walking around and connecting with your employees gives you a better understanding of the workplace dynamic because it allows you to get to know your team. This is crucial.

My *Lean Six Sigma* background comes into play here too. As a leader, when I walk around by myself or with one of my team members, the conversations we have often lead to productivity gains that can benefit the team, the organisation. Creative ideas and suggestions are born from these informal walks and talks. In the Continous Improvement (CI) world, these are called Gemba walks. Get your notepad ready for all the innovative ideas that can come from MBWA! Remember, walking around, talking, and being curious can generate positive feelings and a positive environment.

3. **Open Your Door**

I know what you are thinking: what could having an open door policy possibly mean in today's work environment of shared spaces and open format offices? Well, the literal meaning might no longer work, but the premise is still the same. It means providing transparency and openness with your communications in a way that makes your office a welcoming space for your employees to enter.

I also want to focus on the opportunities for collaboration the open-door policy grants you. In such an open and inviting atmosphere, employees feel emboldened and empowered to suggest ideas, start conversations, and share concerns. In this atmosphere, you and your team will be united by a common purpose and equipped to work toward a common goal. It supports the achievement of a business benefit even as it grants a benefit to the people involved in the organisation. Successful leaders create a collaborative environment such as this one because it fosters trust, and this in turn grants the department the kind of cohesion that makes a successful team. In a cohesive environment where all the employees (as components of an organic system) are connected, knowledge and expertise can readily be shared, and this leads to higher productivity, empathy among employees, and precisely that empowering feeling of success which drives employee satisfaction and engagement.

Remember, employee engagement begins with leadership. It is an indispensable part of a direct manager's job because employees appreciate more the efforts toward engagement made by persons with whom they maintain everyday contact. Only such a manager can cultivate respect, fairness, pride, and camaraderie that define an organisational culture of engagement. Because timing is very important, managers must quickly and actively pursue their team's engagement, recalling that companies whose teams can boast a culture of engagement significantly outperform rivalling organisations that fail to cultivate similar levels of devoted interest in their employees. And while it is true that employee engagement takes tremendous time and effort on the part of the leader, it never fails to be an achievable goal and one that always proves itself worth the effort. Therefore, it can certainly be an achievable objective for your organisation if you remember to build strong and empathic connections between yourself and your employees; engage with them by walking around and letting them know you are alert, aware, and fully there; and maintain an open-door policy that makes them feel welcome in your presence. In such a free, open, and engaging environment, creativity and productivity can thrive.

Definitions

Employee Engagement: The active participation and reinforcement by the management of any organisation to ensure that all employees with a company are happy, healthy, coming up with great and innovative ideas, and generally engaged with their work to the point of performing at their personal best.

Lean Six Sigma: This methodology is based on the practice of minimising waste in the working environment and increasing the productivity of a business, as well as its employees.

Open Door Policy: The physical act of a workplace keeping the doors of all employees with offices open, literally, to constantly invite open communication methods, transparency towards all other employees, as well as clientele and customers, plus to encourage those employees who may want to approach management staff to always know that management is approachable and available to their questions and inquiries and that management are there to help to in order to encourage a positive environment.

Walk Around: The concept of supervisors and front line management staff of an organisation physically walking around a workplace, or if the manager has a physical disability, accessing the workplace via wheelchair as one example, to ensure that there is a constant presence of management staff that presents the authentic image of caring about their employees, to ultimately encourage their employees to care about the given company.

Workplace's Engagement Culture: Although many workplaces require improvements in the workplace's engagement culture, every single working environment does have an engagement culture that may or may not require improvement.

References

Allen, Melanie. "Employee Engagement: A Culture Change."
Insights. The Insights Group, Ltd. 2014. https://www.insights.com/media/1091/employee-engagement-a-culture-change.pdf

Belhadi, A., Kamble, S. S., Zkik, K., Cherrafi, A., & Touriki, F. E. (2020). The integrated effect of Big Data Analytics, Lean Six Sigma and Green Manufacturing on the environmental performance of manufacturing companies: The case of North Africa. *Journal of Cleaner Production, 252*, 119903.

Edmans, Alex. (March 24, 2016). "28 Years of Stock Market Data Shows a Link between Employee Satisfaction and Long-Term Value." *Harvard Business Review*. https://hbr.org/2016/03/28-years-of-stock-market-data-shows-a-link-between-employee-satisfaction-and-long-term-value

Harvard Business Review Analytic Service. (September 2013). "The Impact of Employee Engagement on Performance." *Harvard Business Review*. https://hbr.org/resources/pdfs/comm/achievers/hbr_achievers_report_sep13.pdf

Kaswan, M. S., & Rathi, R. (2020). Investigating the enablers associated with implementation of Green Lean Six Sigma in manufacturing sector using Best Worst Method. *Clean Technologies and Environmental Policy*, 1-12.

Sasser, Jr., Earl. and Frank S. Leonard. (March 1980). "Let First-Level Supervisors Do their Job." *Harvard Business Review*. https://hbr.org/1980/03/let-first-level-supervisors-do-their-job

Scott, Dow, and Tom McCullen. (June 2010). "The Impact of Rewards Programs on Employee Engagement." World at Work: The Total Rewards Association. https://www.worldatwork.org/adimLink?id=39032

Chapter 3: Recognition

Summary: This chapter focuses on the importance of *showing gratitude or appreciation* in a work environment. *Recognition* for an employee's hard work can support engagement so show recognition! Don't be the type of leaders such as a *coward* or a *hero* who is afraid to recognize his team.

This introduces a topic that has always been one of my favourites: *employee appreciation*. The American Heritage dictionary defines appreciation as the "thankful recognition" of another based on the actions they have performed. This definition includes not only *gratitude* but a *public demonstration* of gratitude that leads to the recognition of this act of service not just by the recognizer (you) but by third parties who were also involved in the achievement of the organisation's common objective (Raja Sreedharan, Balagopalan, Murale & Arunprasad, 2020).

Although I have been in the role of team leader, I have also always been an employee; one that has seen, and believes in the importance of appreciating employees. Having spent 20+ years in these roles has equipped me with enough experience and understanding that I can be of help to others in similar situations. It is my goal to help you see the value in the small gestures that add up to making your employees feel like they belong. I aim to make you see that employee appreciation is loaded with benefits, not just for the receiver, but also the organisation as a whole (Sodhi, Singh & Singh, 2020).

Studies done by Berks and Beyond Employee Services, Inc. (BBES) have indicated in its study on organisational leadership, employees engage far more with each other and with the organisation when they are securely integrated into the team, its goals, methods, and culture (2014). Employee recognition boosts employee retention! As BBES states, "Companies using strategic recognition are forty-eight percent more likely to report high engagement" (par. 3). This means workers need not only to be useful but also to feel useful—even indispensable—to the projects undertaken in the company (Son, 2016). This occurs only when employees are in an environment where they don't have to guess that they're appreciated. They feel secure when they have a leader who isn't afraid to show gratitude for a job well done (Raja Sreedharan, Balagopalan, Murale & Arunprasad, 2020).

Now it certainly doesn't require just a leader's appreciation to boost the confidence of an employee—and in fact, your goal should build an organisational culture that fosters warmth, acceptance, and the peer-to-peer expression of gratitude by everyone. But the best way to achieve this is to exemplify it first as the leader.

Employees feel like stakeholders in a business when they feel appreciated, and when that sentiment comes directly from the leader it encourages them to do the same for those around them. Jared Lewis points out that employees are already stakeholders since their livelihood depends on the success of the organisation (Chron, 2019). Lewis indicates that the number one factor in engaging employees' wholehearted support for an organisation's goals is to make them feel like they have a certain amount of ownership—or a stake—in the company (par. 4-5). This results in a more open and welcoming work environment in which employees feel more like their activities make a difference for them too and not just for management. And appreciation makes a difference not just in the workplace but in the lives of the individuals who spend so much of their day in that space.

You might ask: if employee appreciation is so easy and so rewarding, why would anyone ever fail to do it? Let's take a moment to understand why leaders might forfeit this powerful opportunity to capture the loyalty of their employees. An article titled "Declining Employee Loyalty" published in 2012 by the Wharton School of Business cites the difficulty in quantifying the benefits of rewards and recognition for employee loyalty as a significant cause of this failure. I've done my research and identified three types of leaders that might be susceptible to this. Becoming acquainted with these various types will give insight into the situations or personalities that might prompt this devastating omission.

The Coward: While fear is an instinct that has perhaps correctly prompted people to take cover in dangerous situations, most of the time it just keeps us from bigger and better things. Fear of losing status can be crippling in interpersonal relationships between leaders and their subordinates. Studies published in *The Guardian* and *The Muse* support the idea that leaders are often afraid that any appreciative treatment an employee receives over and above wage compensation might lead to jealousy or arrogance (Osborne 2010; Thetford).

But, I ask, So what?! Is there a way for anyone to feel too good? When you appreciate someone, s/he should feel amazing. Feelings of happiness and pride in their competence rarely leads people to engage in obnoxious behaviour. Rather, it leads them to be open and personable. Especially, it leads them to devise more ways to please you and encourages them to take further initiatives that can enhance the workspace and the business—and their reputations. Examples of this abound. For instance, Susan M. Healthfield's 2016 article for The Balance states that prioritizing employee recognition results in a "positive, productive, innovative organisational climate" (par. 1).

So what could be holding us back? Okay, let's examine a couple of scenarios in which a leader's efforts at recognition might go wrong.

Imagine that Jodie and Stan work together in your department and both perform well in different aspects of an account that leads to a 15% increase in sales. While Jodie identified and pushed the product toward a particular slice of the market that had gone untapped, Stan did the ground research and prepared the reports that allowed her to make decisions about the particular demographic to target. You recognize the efforts made by Jodie and somehow forgot Stan's input. Stan will of course feel slighted that his work went unnoticed and maybe even jealous that Jodie got all the praise (Sodhi, Singh & Singh, 2020).

Jealousy: Hilary Osborne (2010) cites jealousy as a destructive force in the workplace. As a possible cause of employee repression and the lack of appreciation, jealousy is certainly destructive, as it can lead to such mismanagement of the company's human resources. Employees indeed get jealous whenever leaders' standards or criteria for recognition fail to include all how employees contribute to the growth and success of the company. Trying to be inclusive when attempting to understand your employees and the ways they contribute is one way of avoiding jealousy among employees. Also, when communicating these criteria to employees, be specific about the behaviours that will be recognized. Specificity is key, Heathfield (2016) reports when dealing with the disbursement of benefits and recognition in response to employees' performance. Then, once the criteria have been laid out, honour the criteria, and no one should feel left out or jealous. In such a workplace, recognition becomes the asset it truly should be and not a liability.

Okay, so you made that mistake and recognized only Jodie when you should have included Stan. Now ideally Jodie would pick up your slack and extend some of the recognition to the help Stan provided her. But what if Jodie gets carried away with the praise she received yesterday and starts bragging or even slacking off today?

Arrogance

Employers might also fear that employees who get a so-called big head, might become over-confident, and be difficult to deal with in future situations. These fears are legitimate: Thetford's study of workplace dynamics (published on TheMuse.com, 2019) has indeed identified arrogance as a valid concern for leaders and managers in the workplace. Because of this potential for arrogant and insubordinate employees, leaders tend to shy away from making their employees feel too good about the actions they perform. So I have to admit that the chance does exist for confidence to transgress into arrogance; but if such an employee does become unpleasant or over-confident, then as a strong and wise leader, you already have the skills to manage that.

What do you do then? Find a way to recognize Stan next time. Heathfield (2016) suggests that simply asking Stan how he'd like to be recognized is a good way to ensure that your efforts don't go unnoticed. This way, you can make up for the damage you did to Stan's morale and dress Jodie down a notch in the process. Kill two birds! And, truth be told, an unpleasant reaction to gratitude and appreciation says far more about the recipient than it does about you. Be the bigger person. Appreciate sincerely and hope the recipients of your favour can deal with it. Chances are they can, and you and those around you will be the happier for it.

The Hero: In this case, this reaction to the prospect of recognizing others says much about you! It says you're caring, valiant, even chivalrous, but perhaps a bit to a fault. Greg Satell's 2015 article in Forbes states that the position of any leader who aims to heroically control the entire fate of the organisation is increasingly untenable in today's workspaces. He argues that those who insist on being (rather than creating) heroes might be "the most frustrated and bitter" and end up doing "everything you aren't supposed to do in a mature, well-functioning organisation" (par. 18).

This suggests that while a leader should strive to facilitate growth within the organisation and to remove all impediments that would stop the progress of production, too great a desire for heroic behaviour might lead to more harm than good. For instead of seeing, recognizing, and appreciating the values of others, the leader might push too hard for her solutions to be implemented by the team. This drive toward being the hero causes her to ignore the ideas and innovations put forth by her employees and ultimately to compromise not only the effectiveness but also the cohesion of the team. The extreme of this kind of dubious heroism would be a leader who tries to put employees down or even steal their credit. Heroic behaviour can be good but always keep in mind whose hero you're trying to be. If you're there to help your employees, that's a good thing, but there's a chance you might be in it to be a hero for yourself. Be careful not to fall into the trap of selfish heroism and inadvertently become an unscrupulous leader.

Be Everybody's Hero!

This point is related to consistency in dealing with recognition. Don't forget to be thorough when listing employees that deserve praise. Kennedy, a high-level executive who was in charge of several lower-level managers often made speeches at company events. Kennedy admitted that he would stand up with the best of intentions and begin to name persons whose work he was pleased with. But since he did this off-the-cuff and with no list of names prepared beforehand, he would invariably forget to name some of the managers who had done very good work in their departments. Needless to say, the morale of the manager and that of the entire department fell. Bad news for productivity and the overall organisational culture.

Effective Heroes are on Time!

What would happen if Superman came to the rescue a second or two after Lois Lane hit the ground? Splat! Recognize everyone and do it promptly. Don't let them forget why they're being praised. York College (2013) has identified in Millennial employees a need for instant gratification that translates in the workplace as instant recognition for what they have done right. Its author states that leaders need to be "vigilant in their efforts to identify positive Millennial behavior and consistent in their immediate recognition practices" (Managing Millennials par. 11). And this means enabling recognition tools that don't require several layers of approval before they can be implemented.

What if you need several weeks to get approval for an appreciation initiative and you end up recognizing Stan weeks later than when he prepared those amazing reports. Then for all that time in between, he might end up feeling unappreciated and wind up underperforming due to low morale. You can't afford to lose that time. Don't let him forget the act or the attitude that drove him to perform it in the first place.

Some of my workplaces have successfully used peer to peer tools for recognition. Sabrina Son (2016) has cited the use of these peer to peer tools for recognition as an effective method of sharing some of the burdens of employee recognition. Peer-to-peer tools are designed to encourage employees' recognition of their fellow workers, and their use "instills a sense of team spirit, motivates employees to do great work, and promotes openness and transparency" within an organisation (Vranjes 2014, par. 1). This also ensures that recognition gets around to more people. Let someone else be a hero! Providing ways in which fellow employees can recognize their fellows for work well done gives you as an employer a wider perspective from which to view the various activities of the organisation. Son states that 41% of managers using peer-to-peer tools for recognition see increased productivity and customer satisfaction (par 12). And no wonder, because they make it easier to get a handle on who's doing what. With more eyes around, good work and kind deeds get seen and appreciated more regularly. Employees get more individual recognition and feel a sense of belonging to the group. And remember that people want not only to get but to give. Being able to give recognition to motivates employees too. Cicero Group reports that having tools to recognize others motivates 50% of employees.

The Player: Players have maturity issues—we all know that. The managerial "player" is an immature or insecure leader, the type that plays games instead of being straight-forward with employees. Leaders are often tempted to behave like "players" when they are new to the position. While trying to grow into it, they try to find… er… creative methods to drive productivity and engagement or to gain employees' respect. Some might call this kind of negative creativity simply a case of resorting to manipulation or games. As Terri Levine (2007) says, a manager with maturity issues "can sabotage the career paths of those he perceives as a threat to his position" (par. 11). Again, such leaders place the focus on themselves: it's all about them. But this almost always is to the detriment of the team. And as a longitudinal study supported by the Swedish Research Council on the effect of self-centred leaders shows, employees tend to be more depressed and exhibit low morale when their leaders are immature and exhibit the selfish attitudes of a player (Theorell et al. 2012).

What you must understand is that learning to become a good leader takes time, and if you're new to this, it's best to be honest to yourself and your employees when you haven't got everything figured out. Realize that being open and honest with your employees shows them that you trust them, and it helps you gain the experience and maturity required for your position. So yes, you'll grow into it. And chances are if you trust your employees they will work and grow with you. Playing games, on the other hand, simply insults their intelligence, and will likely cause them to lose respect for you. You can't afford to risk that—don't be a player.

Inconsistency, or Don't Play Around with Rewards

Set goals. Then anyone who meets the goals should be recognized, not just the one who exceeds it by the highest amount. If you recognise only the top performer even when others have met the criteria for recognition, you will encourage distrust that leads to laxity and indifference. As Heathfield (2016) has noted, "Recognizing only the highest performer will defeat or dissatisfy all of your other contributors." Fewer employees will bother to try to meet a goal, especially if they think they might be outdone by someone else and therefore never get recognized. If employees think their work is in vain, they won't be motivated to do it. A leader needs everyone on the team to be working, not just a few. So, reward everyone who deserves it.

Opportunity Lost?

So, why is failing to show appreciation for a lost opportunity? What is to be gained by appreciating employees and what exactly do you lose when you don't? Well, besides all the amazing karma.... here are some very practical reasons why employee appreciation is a chance for organisational growth and development that you don't want to forfeit.

1. It Builds Your Employees' Self-confidence

The American Management Association (2019) identifies employee self-confidence as a very significant aspect of cultivating a healthy, productive workforce able to handle and respond well to the caprices of the market and other intra-organisational changes ("Building Employee Confidence"). If you think about it, confidence development makes a lot of sense. Hearing or reading something positive and encouraging about themselves provides a boost to your employees' self-confidence, self-esteem, and overall self-image. Any behavior you show that has that kind of positive result in your employees can't help but motivate them to put in an extra effort for you and the team you lead. Have you ever witnessed the kind of drive a person exhibits when they think they can do something? And wouldn't you rather have a team composed of persons who feel positively driven to do their jobs? A simple act of appreciation can ignite the kind of fire in your team members that encourage them to go all out for the team. Your team! And that's an advantage you can't afford to lose.

2. **It Encourages Employees' Development**

Every time you show your appreciation for a job well done, what you're doing is giving positive and meaningful feedback to your team member. Positive reinforcement encourages employees not only to do a similar job in the future but to strive to do an even better job. Even though this might require the development and hone of their current skills and perhaps the acquisition of new skills, they will be motivated to do this extra work as long as they have the confidence that it will be rewarded. Chronus' (2019) article on career development supports this idea that such efforts "should be self-directed, employee-driven programs that allow employees to help themselves" ("Modernizing Employee Development"). Showing appreciation in open and meaningful ways allows you to cultivate the best traits in your team as well as to motivate each person to develop those missing traits. All of these improve the organisation on three levels: it makes individual team members more successful, strengthens the team and the overall organisation, and shows your leadership to be more effective.

3. **It Builds Relationships:** UC Berkeley's Human Resources (2019) article on career management recognizes relationship building in the workforce as "One of the most important career management habits for career success and resiliency" (par. 1). This pertains to professional relationships occurring between team members as well as between you and each employee. Seeing something of value in your employee, and having the courage and goodwill to share that with him or she strengthens the relationship between you. It lets all your employees know that you're keenly interested in the abilities they bring to the table and are generally paying attention to who's doing what in the department. Strong relationships are indispensable when trying to get jobs done and to attain high goals or standards. And as Esther Derby (2011) indicates, strong relationships should be co-created between managers and employees. When employees get along with each other, they're more likely to collaborate successfully on projects, and whenever you genuinely get along with all employees—without leaving anyone out—

you've taken the first step to ensuring the cohesion of the entire group. Showing the team how and why they should value each of its members is an effective way of leading by example.

4. It Develops Your Influence

When a team member witnesses a public gesture made to show appreciation for something she has done, she feels valued, respected, and indispensable to the organisation. In a mature relationship such as that which you seek to cultivate as a leader, these attitudes will be extended mutually: when you give it, you get it in return. Such reciprocal debts, whether of gratitude or other value, serve "as a stabilizing function" within an organisation or department (Uhl-Bien and Maslyn, 2003, 512). Sincere appreciation engenders respect and trust, your influence with your employees should grow in proportion to the levels of respect and trust you receive from them.

5. It Grants Fulfilment to all Parties

By now you have a better understanding of how appreciation boosts self-image, employee cohesion, and your influence as a leader. And, no doubt you're already aware that authentic appreciation when shown, can make someone's day. This is no trivial effect, and in fact, it makes more than just someone's day: you can make their entire world a better place! This extends far past you and the rest of the persons in your department. Beyond boosting productivity with all the increased engagement employees show as a result (a huge benefit!), a leader who habitually makes an employee's day contributes an overall improvement to the general vibe of the workplace, making it somewhere people want to come to every day. Your workplace then becomes a haven of security and productivity—a great place to run as a leader. But as a human being, this kind of responsibility for the good humour and high morale of your employees benefits you on an emotional level as well, because when you make someone else feel fulfilled, you become fulfilled too. This kind of improved morale will—for all involved—be inevitable, but it will be especially true for you since you live with the knowledge that you've helped to make someone's life better.

So how might a leader go about showing appreciation? One of the easiest ways to begin is with a willingness to express yourself. In particular, whenever you feel gratitude, it's good to show it. It might be even better, however, to articulate the *why* behind your gratitude. This usually requires a bit of thought, and it prevents those automatic and petty gestures like saying, "Sure, thanks" without really making the effort to let your employees know you mean it. Platitudes like that merely mimic gratitude, but only end up seeming empty. On the other hand, a thoughtful expression of gratitude that includes an explanation of why your employee's action was important to you personalizes the gesture and prevents you from seeming glib. It is this kind of intentional gratitude that ends up being more understood and more appreciated in the end. Such well-executed appreciation motivates and gives positive reinforcement that goes a long way to improving the overall culture and productivity of the organisation.

Definitions

Appreciation: A spirit in a work environment where employees feel valued for their hard work every single day.
Gratitude: Employees also feeling grateful for working in a wonderful job environment, and in turn, managers and supervisors fostering the spirit to encourage employees to want to feel grateful for the jobs and the careers that they have.
Public Demonstration: Ensuring that employees who are consistently engaged and do the right things on the path of employee engagement are recognized in front of others for their outstanding behaviours. Typically conducted to encourage more like-minded positive behaviours.
Recognition: Acknowledging employees that are consistently excellent and also begin the path of professional excellence while in the workplace and encouraging an atmosphere where employees feel noticed for their good behaviour.

References

Berks & Beyond. "Employee Recognition Doesn't Matter (or does it?) 4 Statistics that will Make You Rethink Recognition." http://www.berksandbeyond.com/2014/07/08/allentown-staffing-agencies-employee-recognition/

"Building Employee Confidence." (2019). American Management Association. http://www.amanet.org/training/articles/building-employee-confidence.aspx

Career Management-Relationship-Building. (2019). *Human Resources*. UC Berkeley. http://hr.berkeley.edu/development/career-development/career-management/relationship-building

"Declining Employee Loyalty: A Casualty of the New Workplace." (May 9, 2012). Wharton.

The University of Pennsylvania. http://knowledge.wharton.upenn.edu/article/declining-employee-loyalty-a-casualty-of-the-new-workplace/

Derby, Esther. (September 9, 2011). "A Manager's Guide to Building a Relationship with the Team." Esther Derby Associates, Inc.: Designing Your Environment for Agile Success. http://www.estherderby.com/2011/09/creating-relationsips-with-teams.html

Heathfield, Susan. M. (August 11, 2016). "The Power of Positive Employee Recognition." *The Balance.* https://www.thebalance.com/the-power-of-positive-employee-recognition-1919054

Lewis, Jared. (2019). "How Are Employees Affected as Stakeholders." http://smallbusiness.chron.com/employes-affected-stakeholders-38732.html

Levine, Terri. (2019). "What is Wrong with Management

Today?" Terri Levine: The Guru of Coaching. http://www.terrilevine.com/articles/wrong-with-management.htm

"Managing Millennials: It's All About Immediate Recognition." (August 5, 2013). LeHigh Valley Business. http://www.lvb.com/article/20130805/LVB01/308029992/Managing-Millennials:-It%E2%80%99s-all-about-immediate-recognition

"Modernizing Employee Development for Today's Workforce: Why Career Development is More Important than Ever." (2019). Chronos. http://chronus.com/employee-development

Osborne, Hilary. (June 18, 2010). "Envy in the Workplace: Jealous Guise." https://www.theguardian.com/money/2010/jun/19/envy-workplace-recession

Raja Sreedharan, V., Balagopalan, A.,

Murale, V., & Arunprasad, P. (2020). Synergising Lean Six Sigma with human resource practices: evidence from literature arena. *Total Quality Management & Business Excellence, 31*(5-6), 636-653.

Satell, Greg. (October 3, 2015). "True Leaders are Not Heroes. True Leaders Creates Heroes." *Forbes*. https://www.forbes.com/sites/gregsatell/2015/10/03/true-leaders-are-not-heroes-true-leaders-create-heroes/#7e5d13703f13

Sodhi, H. S., Singh, D., & Singh, B. J. (2020). A conceptual examination of Lean, Six Sigma and Lean Six Sigma models for managing waste in manufacturing SMEs. *World Journal of Science, Technology and Sustainable Development*.

Son, Sabrina. (August 4, 2016). "12 Mind-Blowing Stats on Employee Recognition You Need to Know." *Tiny Pulse*... https://www.tinypulse.com/blog/sk-employee-recognition-stats

Theorell, Töres, Anna Nyberg, Constanze Leineweber, Linda L. Magnusson Hanson, Gabriel Oxenstierna, and Hugo Westerlund. (September 24, 2012). "Non-listening and Self-Centered Leadership - Relationships to Socioeconomic Conditions and Employee Mental Health. *Plos One*. http://journals.plos.org/plosone/article?id=10.1371/journal.pone.0044119

Thetford, Caris. (2019). "How to Deal with an Arrogant Co-worker Who Drives You up the Wall." The *Muse*. https://www.themuse.com/advice/how-to-deal-with-an-arrogant-coworker-who-drives-you-up-the-wall

Uhl-Bien, Mary, and John L. Maslyn. (2003). "Reciprocity in

Manager-Subordinate Relationships: Components, Configurations, and Outcomes." *Journal of Management.* Vol. 29, No. 4. 2003. pp. 511-532. https://pdfs.semanticscholar.org/acaf/bdb4914e730cc04d65ef7becad5a742e81a4.pdf

Vranjes, Toni. (October 23, 2014). "Employers Embrace Peer-to-Peer Recognition." *Society for Human Resource Management.* https://www.shrm.org/hr-today/news/hr-magazine/pages/1114-peer-recognition.aspx

Chapter 4: Empowering Leadership

Summary: Teamwork and collaboration are becoming more and more necessary in today's workplace. Trust, respect, autonomy, ownership, and a problem-solving mindset all help to allow a team to achieve its goals. And, an empowering leadership style allows a team leader to share power and cultivate an environment of engagement.

Teams in the Workplace

What is a team? This chapter will give an overview of team development in the workplace and explain my rationale for ***granting that teamwork and collaboration*** play such important roles in an organisation's success. The very definition of a workplace team places the group of employees in a collaborative setting working on a goal that they all share. This may be an ad hoc group—one placed together temporarily for a specific purpose, or it may be a permanent group—one pursuing a task that represents an on-going objective of the company. The former is called a project group (and might also be known as a steering committee or task force), while the latter can be divided into cross-functional teams and self-directed work-teams. Cross-functional teams comprise of employees from various departments within an organisation, while a self-directed team "determines how it will get a job done and has the authority, and often the budget, to carry out decisions" (Dummies, n/a). It would be desirable to have all teams work in a somewhat self-directed way as far as their level of motivation and commitment is concerned. That way, all workplace teams would reflect a high level of engagement, and their effectiveness will be enhanced by deliberate teamwork and purposeful collaboration ("Types of Workplace Teams").

How to Form a Team *Team-building* activities like meals, adventures, training, and ropes activities strengthen the cohesiveness of groups and the level of trust that they share. These activities improve members' willingness and ability to communicate with each other by giving them opportunities to practice communication open and honestly (Ghabra, August 23, 2012). The key to such activities is that they place members in artificially constructed situations whose outcome depends on the speed and accuracy with which they share information among themselves. While the stakes might be low with such concocted tasks, it both encourages and gives employees the space to pursue openness and honesty in their communication with one another. The newly formed relationships can then be brought with them to real, workplace situations in which the stakes—and the rewards—are higher. As Dwain Richardson (February 2016) puts it, "if other benefits are achieved through team building, like better communication, this will ultimately lead to stronger results."

Stages of Team Development

Team developers have used the *five stages of forming, storming, norming, performing, and transforming* to gauge the progress of team building (Heathfield, 2016). After the initial stages of persons gathering to make the group (forming), a period of disorder ensues (storming) in which they might express a lack of consensus on the team's goals and vision. This occurs while they get to know each other. Once the leader guides the group through this stage and facilitates clarity about vision and relationship building, they enter a period of norming in which they can make progress toward goals. At this point, steady work is done based on the plans made in this norming stage and the team starts performing. Once this goal is achieved, the team must transform itself (whether drastically or minimally) to fit its capacities to new objectives discovered along the way (Heathfield, 2016).

Hallmarks of an Empowered and Engaged Team

Empowering leadership involves granting the tools, confidence, and the authority to one's subordinates to encourage their creativity and initiative, and to groom them for future leadership. ***Empowerment*** is the very act of according power to another, and it supports engagement since the ***empowering qualities of autonomy, responsibility, and ownership*** (also ***tenets of engagement***) aid in building trust and respect and drives a problem-solving mindset—the two other aspects of engagement. According to the Plumbline Management Corporation's (2011) series on strategic market leadership, the empowerment of one's employees is critical to the organisation's development. As such:

"The empowerment approach stresses that the wisdom, skill, and experience of individual team members are essential resources for the organisation. Therefore, individual contribution is highly valued by leadership. With this style, measurable goals are set up by agreement between leadership and participants, responsibility is assigned to each individual, corresponding authority is delegated to carry out tasks, and deadlines for review and assessment are set" (Empowerment Leadership, 2011).

Employee teams are critical to your business, so once they form it becomes important not only to ensure that they are empowered and engaged but to know exactly what it is that makes an engaged team. This ensures that you will be aware when your team achieves or falls short of this mark. As discussed above, open and honest communication stimulates the capacity for the team to conceive effective and productive plans and see them through to fruition. Such communication places them on a path to healthy growth and encourages them to develop qualities that are the hallmark of any engaged team:

Autonomy: Autonomy describes the ability of a team to be self-directed, to make independent decisions (Leadership Styles, 2011). It reflects a kind of self-motivation, self-assembly, and self-governing that removes any need for constant external stimuli by higher-level management. Such an empowered team is by no means leaderless, but embraces the leader as part of the team and therefore works—with a motivation that comes from within—toward a goal it views as its own. Autonomy thus encourages each member to make a meaningful contribution toward this goal, which involves making better day-to-day decisions about how to act, both individually and collaboratively, so that this objective be met (Robertson, 2019).

Responsibility: The above paragraph suggests that a team's autonomy translates to the team's responsibility for the work and decisions to be made. Yet, rather than reflecting a burden to the team, autonomy-driven responsibility encourages the team to take as its own the objective to be met. It involves accountability—the reluctance to place blame elsewhere and the willingness not just to accept the ramifications of one's actions but also to change course along with the team when things seem to be going awry (Abughosh, April 14, 2015). Such responsibility stems from the high level of empowerment that self-direction grants team members. Because each views the other as an equally responsible member of the group, autonomy discourages selfishness by urging employees toward developing qualities beneficial both to the individual and to the team.
Trust and Respect:

Employees need to view not just their managers as trustworthy but also the other employees they work with as peers. Respect works similarly, and both must be present in a workplace that seeks cohesion among its members. Honesty is the cornerstone of trust, and the ability to use good judgment when deciding the most prudent way to share information comes second. Communication is very important and involves both sharing information that will enhance the team's productivity and cohesion (such as examples of successes or positive behaviour) and suppressing that information which could prove detrimental (such as gossip). Placing as much emphasis on the recognition of others as oneself within the group supports trust and respect, as no single person will be seen as self-seeking; rather each has at heart the interests of others, and the group as a whole (Mayfield, 2019).

Ownership: Neil Kokemuller (2019) emphasizes that employees who have been empowered by their leaders "typically feel a stronger sense of ownership and worth when entrusted to make important decisions" (par. 4). When employees consider themselves as owners or stakeholders of a business, it encourages their retention and improves their performance (NCEO, 2019). This becomes even more beneficial when each employee recognizes both him-/herself and fellow employees as co-claimants to the company and its objectives. In such a situation, a favourable employee culture ensues, one that encourages each member to act with the best of intentions toward the group and its objectives, knowing that the group's cohesion supports the fulfillment of these goals that will ultimately benefit each employee.

A Problem-Solving Mindset: When employees demonstrate their care for the group, they show their willingness and determination to see the operation/business succeed; they are ready to solve business challenges and contribute to business success. Adopting and cultivating a problem-solving mindset provides tremendous benefits to the team, the company, and its bottom line. Harvard's Information for Employees (HARVie, September 22, 2016) defines mindset as "the ideas and attitudes with which a person approaches a situation." Therefore, a problem-solving mindset indicates that, rather than being daunted by difficulties along the road to the company's goals, its employees will always approach them with a view to removing the problem and determining a solution that will facilitate moving toward the team's foreseen objective.

When a team is successful, the leader must recognize the need to reward its members (or the team as a whole) for the job it has performed so well. (See the chapter on recognition). While recognition often comes in terms of tangible and intangible rewards and benefits, it is also important to note that it can also come in the form of more challenging assignments. This falls directly under the style of leadership that empowers people by handing them not only the tools but also the authority to work creatively and independently. Showing a team and its members that you trust them to perform greater challenges is extremely complimentary and is the hallmark of an empowering leader (Leadership Styles, 2011). It rewards employees' sense of accomplishment, their sense of self-efficacy, and it also motivates them to maintain the sense of responsibility which the leader has seen in them—and which the very act of giving them a more challenging assignment shows.

Exemplary Teams

Though it is never an easy feat to get people to work together, lots of companies have still managed to cultivate great engaged teams. How did they do it? Here are some real-world examples of very successful companies that have found creative ways to foster engaged teams, encourage their employees to work well together, and problem-solve their way to business success.

Southwest Airlines has made several advances in using the skills of the entire team to enhance its product and public image. The company has been known to appeal to employees from all departments for input in such innovations that affect the whole group—going, for instance, outside the design department to get ideas for uniforms to engage aspects of employees' creativity that might not have been tapped in the department to which they properly belong. The airline has also used its employees' unconventional skills to its advantage, as is shown in a video of one Southwest team member rapping its airline safety procedures (Holmes). By publicizing this spontaneous act of creativity on the part of an employee, Southwest shows its commitment to seeking out and rewarding the innate abilities of its team members—thereby cultivating a more welcoming and engaging work environment (Maier, December 28, 2016).

Dreamworks gives its employees room for creativity by allowing them to publicize their projects in group spaces. Such sharing of personal information encourages solidarity among Dreamworks' employees, as the courage it takes to share requires trust in the persons who hear these ideas. Such efforts demonstrate "the value of integrating employee engagement into daily company culture" and—more importantly—the value of doing this at the level of the small group. Dreamworks' effort at building trust among employees—by boosting their confidence and assuring them that their ideas matter—shows how much this very successful company values team building (Maier, December 28, 2016).

I cannot stress enough the benefits of transferring responsibility to teams and team members with demonstrated successes as a means of rewarding them. Rather than identifying the "potential" in each member and then trying to fit it into the objectives of the team, I aim to identify the "passion, skills and abilities" of each member -- trying to understand what's important to them and what makes them tick -- and then matching that to what's important in the business/business objectives. I recognized that as a team leader, I ought to be the main link to the company's employee resources and that link needs to be strong—based on trust, appreciation, communication, and diligence—to drive employee retention and productivity. I employed lean philosophy to rally support for the company goals, to demonstrate that these goals were in the interest of the employees, and to define the steps we all would need to take to achieve them. As a team leader, I also strove to communicate transparently so that employees felt secure and informed in their work environment. Finally, I was also keen to celebrate the successes of the department and its employees, as a means of identifying the potential of each team member and of encouraging those behaviours that contributed to the overall success of the department.

Finding and utilising the potential in each member of the group is critical to building engaged teams. I endorse this to enhance the engagement of all the teams of which I have since been a part—whether as a leader or a member. This has required understanding each employee and knowing what their strengths are—and though it takes a huge time investment, it has been more than worth it. As Glen Llopis reminds us, "Employees respect leaders that allow them to use their most natural skills and characteristics." He also points out that such employees "are most engaged when they don't feel confined to an environment of limitations and constraints." Opening up the realm of possibilities for the team allows each member to find the most natural ways they might contribute to the goal—ways that use their talents and skills to maximise the team's potential and ultimately its output.

Definitions

Empowerment: Understanding the importance of an employer's perspective to empower the employees within an organisation to ensure the top levels of success from employees that are desired.

Empowering Leadership: Management of any company and/organisation ensuring that their employees are driven and motivated to feel empowered and to work in an empowering way by setting standards of leadership and mentorship and examples of a strong work ethic.

Empowering Qualities of Autonomy, Responsibility, and Ownership: Autonomy, giving workers the space to make their own positive and productive decision-making for their job tasks, as well as providing them with responsibilities that link with the strengths and their attributes, then ties into responsibilities, as well as providing employees with ownership of their job responsibilities to improve not only their credibility in their jobs but as well as their consistently high-performance levels, as well as their overall confidence in their jobs.

Five Stages of Forming, Storming, Norming, Performing, and Transforming: The five stages of forming, storming, norming, performing, and transforming are used in team-building activities to form strong group dynamics, making the excellence of the team a norm, striving and achieving high-performance levels, as well as transforming the beginning stages of a team into one of greater power and strength for the collective good of the company's goals.

Granting Teamwork and Collaboration: Granting teamwork and collaboration among employees ensures that there are collective camaraderie and group responsibility for the job tasks of both big, small, and daily projects on the job.

Team-building: The act of ensuring that a team is strong and built to last so that backsliding is greatly decreased among the company's employees group, as well as ensuring that rather than a "one for all," mindset is in place among a workforce, that an "all for one," is the dominant mindset.

Team Developers: Team developers are the key people who help to build successful team building.

Tenets of Engagement: The tenents of engagement ensure that there are understood agreements and either written and/or unwritten policies in place within an organisation to ensure that employees are engaged with their job tasks every single day on the job.

References

Abughosh, Suha. (April 14, 2015). "Responsibility and Accountability Should Work Together REALLY!!!" Linked In: Pulse. https://www.linkedin.com/pulse/responsibility-accountability-should-work-together-really-abu-ghosh-5993785093456408576

"Empowerment Leadership – Releasing the Talent of the Team." (October 19, 2011). *Strategic Market Leadership*. Plumbline Management Corporation https://www.plumblinemanagement.com/blog/empowerment-leadership-%E2%80%93-releasing-talent-team

Ghabra, Zaina. (August 23, 2012). "Six Quick Teamwork Games to Engage Employees at Work." *Refresh Leadership*. http://www.refreshleadership.com/index.php/2012/08/quick-games-engage-employees-work/

HARVie. "Problem Solving Mindset."

(September 22, 2016). *Harvard Information for Employees*. https://hr.harvard.edu/event/problem-solving-mindset

Heathfield, Susan M. (March 1, 2017). "What Are the Stages of Team Development?" The *Balance*. https://www.thebalance.com/what-are-the-stages-of-team-development-1919224

Holmes, David. (2019). "Southwest Airlines Safety Rap." https://www.youtube.com/watch?v=fNU0M2dG5h8

Kokemuller, Neil. (2019). "The Concept of Empowerment in Leadership." *Chron*. http://smallbusiness.chron.com/concept-empowerment-leadership-15371.html

"Leadership Styles – Be an Empowering Leader." (September 6, 2011). CEO of Leadership. http://www.smbceo.com/2011/09/06/leadership-styles-be-an-empowering-leader/

Llopis, Glenn. (February 2, 2015). "6 Things

Wise Leaders Do to Engage their Employees." *Leadership*. https://www.forbes.com/sites/glennllopis/2015/02/02/6-things-wise-leaders-do-to-engage-their-employees/#26359f8b7f5d

Maier, Steffen. (December 28, 2016). "5 Companies Getting Employee Engagement Right." *Entrepreneurs*. https://www.entrepreneur.com/article/285052

Mayfield, Pat. (2019). "How to Build Trust in the Workplace." Monster Worldwide. https://www.monster.com/career-advice/article/6-steps-to-building-trust-in-the-workplace-hot-jobs

NCEO. (2019). "A Conceptual Guide to Employee Ownership for Very Small Businesses." NCOE. National Center for Employee Ownership. https://www.nceo.org/articles/employee-ownership-very-small-businesses

Nohria, Nitin, Boris Groysberg, Linda-Eling Lee. (July to August 2008). "Employee Motivation: A Powerful New Model." *Harvard Business Review*. https://hbr.org/2008/07/employee-motivation-a-powerful-new-model

Richardson, Dwain. (February 2016). "12 Benefits of Team Building in 2016." Corporate Challenge Events. https://www.corporatechallenge.com.au/blog/12-benefits-team-building-2016

Robertson, Tanya. (2019). "The Effects of Autonomy on Job Satisfaction." *Chron*. http://work.chron.com/effects-autonomy-job-satisfaction-14677.html

"Types of Workplace Teams." (n/a). *Dummies*. http://www.dummies.com/business/human-resources/workplace/the-types-of-workplace-teams/

Chapter 5: Communication is Critical

Summary: ***Communication*** is a critical aspect of business strategy, whether it is for sharing the vision, tactics, and directives or for building internal cohesion. Here, we will see the benefits of various communication forums and how they can get the attention of your employees; including communicating to employees from certain generations as their communications preferences differ.

While communication can be achieved using a ***top-down (one-way) model***, a ***two-way model of communication*** more efficiently builds the cohesion of the organisation—both internally and externally. According to the top-down model, high-level decision-makers send directives down to subordinates or the company sends its messages to potential customers. Two-way communication improves on this by adding the ability to gather feedback from employees and consequently to improve not just the content of messages but also the mechanism for disseminating information throughout the company.

Communication is critical to employee engagement and by extension to the company's continued existence and profitability. It comes in a variety of suits—not just through the use of words but also via gestures. Therefore, leaders must be careful to coordinate various methods to ensure that a positive and coherent message is being circulated about the organisation. Development of focused communication strategies supports this, enabling you as a leader to share your message—the company's message—and drive a general alignment of actions among employees so the company's overall objectives can be achieved.

The most important resource at a company's disposal is the workforce it employs. Its **employee resources** represent a significant investment, and the health of the organisation depends on the strength of professional relationships between these employees and their managers. This in turn relies on the way the organisational culture facilitates communication of expectations and objectives. An employee that is engaged with the company is almost by definition in constant interaction with the other components of the organisation, and this involves ongoing communication with leaders and other members of the team. We have already seen in chapter one how important internal communication is to a company. Dr. Ritika Srivastava (2019) insists that a strategically defined plan for internal communications "is the lifeblood of any company and the engine that drives employee engagement." He also reinforces the notion that communication ought not to be one way, and by defining a method that establishes a two-way communication flow between higher and lower-level team members, one can ensure that messages and responses flow freely and consistently from top to bottom as well as from bottom to top.

Yet, communication is best practiced when it is focused so that information is not disseminated haphazardly. Managers should, for instance, regulate the frequency of their communication, as a high frequency of messages might create an overload of information that is difficult for employees to process. Instead, streamlining communication so that the correct messages get sent to the appropriate people will reduce the need for employees to sift through loads of information in search of the bits that are relevant to their position in the company. This strategy is simply a variation on a rule of thumb used in rhetoric—that of understanding one's audience. Knowing which employees need which portions of information and having the appropriate means of disseminating it goes a long way in making the company's internal communications mechanism run smoothly.

The means of communication are also very important to a company, and they should be varied, sophisticated, and accessible to the entire workforce. The accessibility of communication refers to the appropriateness of the various types of communication to the abilities of the persons expected to benefit from the information it provides. This accessibility objective can be greatly aided by offering a variety of communication methods that allow employees to choose how they communicate. Yet it is also important to remember that granting employees a variety of communication channels to choose from means nothing unless they feel comfortable passing along information in the organisation. Regardless of how sophisticated and robust the communications system, an employee that feels threatened by the prospect of providing the sensitive information to his/her peers or superiors will decline to use the resource. The workplace should therefore be a safe space in which communication is encouraged and never threatened (Srivastava, 2019).

It has been said throughout this book that communication must be open and honest within teams, and this begins with the example of candour that must be set by the team leader. Team leaders that openly express their expectations and offer useful assessments of their subordinates will more readily see progress and development according to their communicated objectives. Such incentives as rewards, benefits, praise—and even censure—are methods of communication that encourage or discourage behaviours by *letting employees know* the extent to which the manager appreciates their actions. Good managers communicate these ideas from the beginning—even at the stage of each prospective employee's interview—by making clear the requirements of the position and communicating the general culture in which the person will be expected to work.

Communicating with Different Generational employees:

Certain generations, for instance, respond better to different forms of communication, and managers should use all those forms to get the attention of all employees.

The *silent generation* prefers face-to-face communication, and while some lower-level employees will be a part of this group, members of this generation often inhabit the role of managers and executives. The challenge will usually be for these persons (as leaders) to find ways of communicating effectively with younger generations who are more technologically oriented. The *baby boomers* do appreciate face-to-face interactions and direct mail, but will also respond to correspondence sent by email. As a result, while certain repeating messages can be sent out to these employees as memos either in soft or hard copy, the one-on-one communication methods should be emphasized for this group.

While ***Generation X*** employees continue to appreciate team meetings and drop-ins to their/your office, much can be accomplished via business communication services that use a social media approach to disseminate messages (whether as texts or as graphic notifications or reminders). They will also respond well to social events. Members of Generation Y (aka ***Millennials***) remain almost constantly plugged into social media or other communication applications. These persons prefer interactive entertainment (social media, video games) rather than the one-directional flow of television and radio. Therefore, communication with employees in this group should allow the real-time flow of information in both directions, yet be mediated through technology. Business software that mimics the effects of such interactive applications should be adopted and utilized. Chances are, Generation Y employees will automatically become plugged into this technology as long as it is available for their use. Therefore, constant communication pathways, once created, have a high likelihood of becoming self-sustaining. Diversifying communication systems to include methods used by all these groups will be of immense benefit to any organisation (Soroptimist, May 2010). Some diverse methods of communication include:

- *One-on-one meetings*: these build stronger relationships between managers and employees and provide an efficient way to check in on the progress of the smaller tactics and strategies that comprise the team's overall objectives. It has the added benefit of allowing managers to give personal feedback, criticize employees without embarrassment, and to praise them personally for their good work and loyalty. These meetings should be scheduled (weekly, biweekly) for *each* member of the team so that no single meeting will arouse suspicion or be dreaded by employees (Atiim, 2019).

- *Team meetings*: these allow managers to share information that pertains to several employees at once. In this way, if a manager finds herself repeating the same directives in various one-on-one meetings, team meetings provide a more efficient alternative. This kind of meeting also encourages teamwork—a crucial aspect that drives the success of any organisation. Gathering employees together in one place allows them to act as a think tank for various concerns of the company. The process of brainstorming ideas becomes more productive, as employees' can bounce concepts off each other and build on each other's ideas. Finally, team meetings allow feedback to occur in real-time and on a broader scale, expediting the process of problem-solving (Belcher, 2019).

- *Town Hall meetings*: these collect together the members of all the several teams that comprise a larger-sized organisation. Townhall meetings, by involving all employees, enjoy all the benefits of team meetings, as stated above: promotion of teamwork, real-time and unfiltered feedback, and facilitation of updates that involve all employees. Additionally, town hall meetings bring employees into contact with leaders at the highest levels of the company and create a level of visibility for that leader that assures employees that someone capable is at the organisation's helm. It helps employees to see the bigger picture, as members of various departments will encounter information about other departments and be better able to see how their work fits into the whole. The town hall meeting can also show employees better ways of practicing the company's values and thereby better integrating them into its overall culture. Seeing high-level executives engage in the same communication processes reinforces the importance of this aspect of the organisation's leadership strategy (EPM, 2017).

- *On their turf*: Since communicating with employees on their turf involves getting to know the type of information and rewards that most inspire each employee, its achievement seems difficult. Yet the rewards are plenty because knowing the kinds of communication and recognition that are most likely to get through to your employees ensures that they truly *understand* your message whenever you send it. Though one might scour an employee's HR file to locate his/her hobbies and passions, true knowledge of one's employee simply cannot be achieved unless one fulfills the requirements of the one-on-one meetings (Langford, February 15, 2016). In short, putting in the time to get to know one's employees provides an immediate and measurable payoff.

- *Knowing one's client*: this method involves understanding the demographic group into which s/he falls. Most workers today use technology to some degree. Some are, of course, familiar with a wider range of technology, some of which involves telecommunication devices. These ubiquitous devices allow communication in real-time and should be harnessed as a tool for improving the culture of communication to bolster the cohesion of one's team. The capabilities provided by mobile phones and social media applications are strong reasons for using these tools.

Definitions

Baby Boomers: Flexible enough to be able to interact with face-to-face communication, direct mail, as well as email.

Communication: Imparting knowledge and/or information.

Diversity: A workforce, or any given situation, where there are groups of people involved from a variety of cultural groups, religious groups, sexual orientations, gender diversity, etc., that contribute in a diverse way to the company's objectives and goals, including managerial and executive positions.

Generation X: Enjoy communication that surrounds team meetings.

Human Resources: This is the department of any given organisation that hires all of the key staff within an organisation internally, as well as externally.

Millennials: Are highly plugged into communication methods linked to social media.

Positive Message: A positive message is one that sends out a sense of hope even when messages may need to be negative, and are always clearly optimistic with indications of even potential improvement to strive for more, when positive.

Silent Generation: Prefer communication that is face-to-face.

Stakeholders: Stakeholders are the key players that are involved with any given organisation that are a vital part of not only the socially responsible aspects of the organisation, but, also the financial aspects of the organisation.

Top-down (one-way) Model: This is a form of communication where a person within an organisation delivers their messages of communication to the person and/or people in which they are speaking to without any invitations of feedback from those receiving the communication messages.

Two-way Model of Communication: With a two-way model of communication, the communication between the main deliverer of the information as well as the recipient(s) is so fluid and interchangeable that it then becomes difficult upon observation to determine who is the deliverer of the communication messages and who is the recipient, depending on the physical surroundings of where the communication situation is being conducted.

References

Atiim. (2019). "6 Benefits of One-on-One Meetings." *Business Goals and Data-Driven Performance Management.* https://www.atiim.com/the-benefits-of-one-on-one-meetings/

Belcher, Lynda Moultry. (2019). "Advantages & Disadvantages of Team Meetings." *Chron.* http://smallbusiness.chron.com/advantages-disadvantage-business-meetings-22125.html

EPM. (2017). "Townhall Meetings: Definition, Advantages and Disadvantages." *Expert Programming Management.* https://expertprogrammanagement.com/2017/11/town-hall-meetings/

Langford, Chad. (February 15, 2016). "Meet

Them on Their Turf: The New Face of Corporate Communications is Interactive." *Training Industry.* https://trainingindustry.com/articles/workforce-development/meet-them-on-their-turf-the-new-face-of-corporation-communications-is-interactive/

Lorette, Kristie. (2019). "Importance of Good Communication in Business." *Chron.* http://smallbusiness.chron.com/importance-good-communication-business-1403.html

Soroptimist International of the Americas. (May 2010). "Communicating Across the Generations." *Soroptimist: Best for Women.* https://www.soroptimist.org/members/membership/membershipdocs/recruitreten/commacrossgen-may2010.pdf

Srivastava, Rikita. (2019). "Role of Communication in Employee Engagement." *People Matters.* https://www.peoplematters.in/article/employee-engagement/role-of-communication-in-employee-engagement-14496

Chapter 6: Get them Involved

Summary: Get your employees involved in the operation by seeking their opinions, ideas, and solutions. Team leaders can leverage experimentation to reap employees' best ideas. And, as an empowering leader, allow your employees to develop these ideas and even be part of the process to see these ideas become reality. This permits growth and deeper understanding that supports continued engagement.

As has already been asserted, an important aspect of empowering leadership is granting authority to another member of the team one leads. ***Experimentation*** is a current trend in business management that empowers employees to be innovative—to think outside the box. It is crucial to realize that this granting of power to another does not diminish your role as a leader. On the contrary, it is possible to retain a great deal of influence after having given the power to a subordinate. Empowering others, rather than diminishing your influence as a manager, *empowers you right back*. Granting decision-making capabilities to other employees boosts their confidence and engagement, while at the same time it gives managers the freedom to properly oversee the bigger picture. It also gives them more opportunities to know their employees and engage with them on a mutually professional (as opposed to a merely hierarchical) level. When managers truly understand their employees' strengths and weaknesses, they know the types of tasks or projects in which each employee's special skills will shine. Such managers know who will do the best job in each area and consequently will *assign* project leadership positions accordingly, not only end up with more robust and innovative products but also with more capable and confident teams.

While managing a team using hands-on methods is appropriate in some situations, leaders do need to resist the temptation to micro-manage. Empowering leadership is one tool that helps avoid this kind of nit-picky management, as it identifies the various smaller areas in which employees are capable and relieves the manager of the need to focus energies at that level. This enabling leadership style not only means letting go of these smaller strands of authority, but it means giving employees the freedom to step in and insert their creativity. Empowering leadership recognizes the differences in the ways people approach problems and projects as a positive ingredient for the blossoming of a creative team that produces innovative products for a diverse market. To a manager used to be the sole leader, the differences another person brings to the task might at first seem strange to the accustomed way of thinking/acting. However, the fresh perspective may be what is necessary to solve a sticky problem or lead production in a new direction that vastly benefits the company and its customers.

Employee empowerment is deeply connected to employee engagement because it looks beyond the subordination of an employee and sees through to the value or *worth* of each (Cucuzza, September 6, 2011). In other words, it forgets that an employee works *for* a company or supervisor and recognizes his/her ability to work *with* others (including the manager) to get the company's goals accomplished. This kind of cooperative culture is what enabling is all about. It renders the manager's job that of a coach who encourages all members of the team to produce according to their strengths and to lead others according to their abilities and expertise.

According to MIT's (2019) human resources research collection, leadership by coaching is a "consultative and participative leadership style" that should be employed by companies "that want to capitalize on the knowledge-base of employees" (Johnson, 2019). To utilize its methods, managers have to accept the assumptions that reinforce the coaching paradigm. Coaching recognizes employees as persons who desire success in their roles. It recognizes that they have much to offer regarding how the company's objectives get accomplished. Coaching also assumes that once employees have been contributors to the drafting of a company objective, they will work hard to ensure that those objectives are realized. Finally, this paradigm assumes that when employees understand how new ideas and methods benefit them, they become open to learning these ideas. Recognition and encouragement of such qualities lead to greater trust in workplaces and, as research shows, "when a manager operates under these assumptions, employees respond positively" (Johnson, 2019).

As coaches, managers encourage three important developments in their employees' professional growth. They *provide direction* that leads directly to *improved performance*, which finally *opens up further possibilities* for the employees to develop as leaders themselves (Johnson, 2019). Getting their attention via communication and appreciation allows employees to have the information necessary to think of ideas that improve operations. Managers provide direction by communicating *at the outset,* the organisation's values, vision, and objectives. When employees understand the company's vision well enough to identify the link between their work and its success, they become motivated to create measures that help them overcome obstacles to these shared goals. In doing this, they will be able to recognize the success of the company as one for themselves as well. Thus, their performance will improve and this will be greatly helped when coaches "provide a 'safe' environment for creativity and risk-taking" (Johnson, 2019). Such an environment does not cast blame and mete out punishment for failures. Rather, it recognizes such setbacks as opportunities for individuals (and the organisation as an *organism*) to learn, to discover, to adjust, and become stronger. And since managers should behave like coaches that support problem-solving and decision making in their employees, in even these difficult situations, coaches can probe their employees in the right ways. For only with the right questions and challenges can they move in the direction necessary to overcome setbacks and learn to be team players that participate in the decisions affecting the company.

Twenty-first-century leadership styles are empowering leadership styles. Millennial employees have been more exposed to collaborative learning and working environments than to the top-down leadership models of the former generations. They think that since everyone has ideas and everyone will be affected by a company's decisions, all should be considered and *consulted* when making a decision. Millennials are concerned with the type of *culture* an organisation's managers cultivate via their methods of leadership. They respond positively to empowering leadership styles. Therefore, in addition to the culture of inclusion and empowerment cultivated by granting decision-making capabilities to employees, the company also benefits from a decrease in dissatisfaction about their roles. According to Peter Stark, when employees are treated as associates with deciding votes, they "focus more of their energy on future-oriented problem solving rather than blaming their current problems on management." When they are left out of decisions, any difficulties that arise are often met by comments emphasizing that it was not their idea or with reasons why such a method cannot work. For many reasons, it would be better to have them air their alternate ideas or their assessments of the plan *before* it is executed. One reason is to understand employees' objections so that valid one can be noted and solutions found that will strengthen the plan. Another reason to share decisions before their execution is so that once a plan has been put into place, employees will support it with the full force of a team that agrees with the direction in which its tasks are going. Thus, if even this plan fails, the members of the team are less likely to place the blame on management but are instead more likely to work together to assess what went wrong and generate new ideas on how to proceed.

An example of a company that has mastered the art of including employees in its decisions is the 3M Corporation. This company has consistently received awards for innovation and has the revenue increases to prove it. Harvard Business Review (2019) assesses that 3M has been "consistently highly ranked [...] in *Fortune* magazine's annual survey of "America's Most Admired Companies." The review also notes that 3M's gross margin and return have over 20 years, averaged 51% and 29% respectively (Srinivas and Govindarajan, August 6, 2013). One of their major strengths lies in their treatment of employees who show promise. It encourages these employees by having regular forums in which they can air their ideas and release them into a pool of workable methods from which the company will draw its plans. Their Centres for Innovation are permanent spaces and structures that provide support for employees' ideas.

The 3M Corporation also encourages employee resourcefulness by offering *seed capital* to those who articulate promising ideas for projects and products. Seed capital is given to employees by their managers to fund ideas within the department itself. However, 3M also offers support and funding for the formation of entirely new business ventures and this encourages employee decision making at the highest level because it allows them to become entrepreneurs. New venture formation grants the monies and capital necessary for employees to *create their businesses* surrounding the products they conceive, and it offers a safety net so that if that product does not make it on the market, the team members can recover their previous jobs. In this way, 3M encourages the kind of calculated risk-taking that is a part of any enterprise and places employees in a position of leadership that grants them higher levels of responsibility and confidence. William McKnight, as chairman of the board, expressed 3M's philosophy brilliantly. He challenges employers: "Encourage experimental doodling. If you put fences around people, you get sheep. Give people the room they need." As seen in the 3M example, employee ideas can mean the start of something very big.

Experimentation in the area of employee autonomy drives innovation, process improvement, and productivity savings in the workplace (Ferrier, 2019). In conventional organisations, while managers did look to employees for novel ideas, the privilege to develop them was often handed off to an "expert team" that would do research and development in their separate departments. This developmental model is inadequate in an organisation that seeks to build a culture of autonomy because it fails to grant "innovation ownership" to the employees whose ideas support these innovations (Ferrier, 2019). Let's face it: no one wants to feel as if their ideas have been stolen and given over to be developed by others who might not care as much about their idea. Instead, bringing together development and innovation (on the one hand) with the generation of ideas (on the other) ensures that the employees have a chance to nurture the plans and therefore *own and support* rather than *resist* the organisational strategies that must be implemented as a result of these innovations. Furthermore, when research and development are integrated into a collaborative work environment, the employees within can communicate ideas more freely and therefore will have access to the information that will help them do their job more effectively.

Finally, experimentation with employee ownership contributes a great deal to an organisation's bottom line. Research done by Rachel Wilcox (March 2, 2016) supports this. This research indicates that in any company, "a more inclusive form of ownership will be attractive to both its employees and clients, and ultimately benefit the bottom line." Using this model, the top-ten United Kingdom accountancy firm Grant Thornton Inc. expects to "double profitability by 2020" and Patrick Lewis, Oxley's finance director, considers this model one that grants a significant "competitive advantage" on many fronts (Wilcox, March 2, 2016). 3M Corporation's methods, too, have shown that allowing employees greater freedom to make decisions increases company revenue. To begin with, when employees are involved in decision and innovation processes, the company saves money it would have expended on outsourcing to consultants (Anderson, April 13, 2018). Also, because employees already understand the inner workings of the organisation, using their knowledge and expertise in the innovation process saves time that would have been spent providing background information to an outsider. This time also translates to money and by extension to a company's revenue.

By entrusting one's employees with important decision-making capabilities, managers allow for growth, understanding, and self-direction in their departments. Employees will take initiative more often and new, valuable, and lucrative projects will get jump-started and flourish under the stewardship of such open managers. Allowing employees to innovate and even express entrepreneurial behaviours—experimentation, or work-time spent on unstructured projects—takes a page out of the leaves of startups, which distribute entrepreneurial or think-tank responsibilities across a relatively wider base of experts and consequently experience faster growth (Cates, May 11, 2018). Thus, the experience of employee empowerment is one of development at micro and macro levels, as it grants managerial experience at the micro level to lower employees and frees managers to focus on more macroscopic, global aspects of the organisation's running.

Definition

Experimentation: Trying new things in the workforce to deliver the best to employees and to encourage employee engagement.

References

Anderson, Casey. (April 13, 2018). "The Advantages of Employee Involvement in Decision Making." *Chron.* http://smallbusiness.chron.com/advantages-employee-involvement-decision-making-18264.html

Cates, Jeff. (May 11, 2018). "Five Ways to Foster a Culture of Experimentation." *Leadership Lab.* The *Globe and Mail.* https://www.theglobeandmail.com/report-on-business/careers/leadership-lab/five-ways-to-foster-a-culture-of-experimentation/article15987469/

Cucuzza, Susan. (September 6, 2011). "Leadership Styles: Be an Empowering Leader." *CEO of Leadership.* Small Business CEO. http://www.smbceo.com/2011/09/06/leadership-styles-be-an-empowering-leader/

Ferrier, Anthony. (May 15, 2018).

"Increasing Innovation and Autonomy Capability: The New Corporate Innovation Imperative." *Strategies*. innovation management. http://www.innovationmanagement.se/2018/03/15/increasing-experimentation-and-autonomy-capability-the-new-corporate-innovation-imperative/

Govindarajan, Vijay, and Srikanth Srinivas. (August 6, 2013). "The Innovation Mindset in Action: 3M Corporation." *Harvard Business Review*. https://hbr.org/2013/08/the-innovation-mindset-in-acti-3

Johnson, Alyce. (2019). "What is Coaching?" *Learning and Development*. MIT | Human Resources. http://hrweb.mit.edu/learning-development/learning-topics/leading/articles/what-is-coaching

Stark, Peter. (February 1, 2010). "6 Reasons to Involve Employees in Decision Making." *Leadership*. Peter Barron Stark Companies. https://peterstark.com/key-to-engagement/

Wilcox, Rachel. (March 2, 2016). "How to Make Employee Ownership Work." *Economia.* https://economia.icaew.com/features/march-2016/how-to-make-employee-ownership-work

Chapter 7: Lean Tools

Summary: The use of Lean tools in the workplace can give a company a competitive advantage - driving down costs and increasing profits. Lean philosophy gives employees the ability to understand the components of the organization's goals and to gauge how well their contribution is working toward the achievement of those goals. Linking lean tools with lean management ideas find employee's strengths and put them to good use, thereby getting the best out of all the company's resources.

Lean tools underscore the need to find profitable ways of providing customer satisfaction in a successful organisation (LMF, 2019). It developed from the perspective that all efforts within an organisation should provide value to the consumer and that no project should be undertaken that fails to have that goal in mind. Lean can give a company, unit, or department a competitive advantage, and it promises results to the bottom line by driving down costs while improving profits. At the production level, Lean hinges on a five-part process of creating a valuable product that revolves around the needs of the customer (Kanban, 2019). These five levels include:

- identifying value
- recognizing the value stream
- managing a continuous workflow
- creating a pull system
- maintaining momentum by continuously improving the production machine.

These levels are briefly outlined below.

Identifying the value (i.e. the product or service) that a customer needs and which the company can provide is followed by a further identification of a ***value stream***. This stream is represented by the various manufacturing departments within the company and a good managerial understanding of how every department can be deeply integrated into the process of producing that value for the customer. The efficiency of this value stream depends on management's ability to integrate production steps that are working and cut (or re-appropriate) those which are not. This leads directly to the creation of a ***continuous workflow***, one whose parts run smoothly together like a well-serviced machine. Once this ease of production is established, it becomes necessary to *create a pull system* that grants to the machine the ability to tailor itself to the changes in demand—that is, it creates a system that optimizes production by manufacturing products only when the need for them arises. Thus, waste is eliminated. The fifth and final step is revisionist, as it emphasizes the continuous improvement of this process. Thus, the cycle never ends, but through a process of *kaizen* or *continuous improvement*, returns to its beginning to ensure that the value (product or service) being provided is always the correct one and the methods used to provide this value are always the most efficient (Kanban; Mulholland).

Examples of lean tools are 5S, key performance indicators (KPI), and root cause analysis (RCA) and these are just as relevant to lean management when one translates their tenets into managerial terms. The knowledge and understanding of these tools can help employees see where their performance fits in the grand production scheme and drive their efforts to engage further with the project (Kaizen, 2019). 5S refers to *sort, shine, set in order, sustain,* and *standardize* and can be implemented to achieve "a clean, uncluttered and well-organised workspace" (Brady, February 2012, 2). *Sorting* (S1) facilitates the identification of essential and non-essential tools/tasks so that the former can be integrated into production and the latter discarded. Shine (S2) involves ensuring that those tasks (or positions or tools) that have been retained are kept always understood and executed efficiently. *Setting in order* (S3) builds on the first two steps, gauging ways of reducing waste and eliminating further sources of clutter, superfluous material, or position duplication—all of which can be generated as part of the production process.

Standardization (S4) establishes the foregoing methods as the rule for running the facility and is implemented once the first three steps have been checked and rechecked to ensure that the methods they advocate are optimal to the facility. *Sustain* (S5), exists to "maintain the momentum generated during the initial event or project" that supported the development of the previous four (Brady p. 14).

Key performance indicators or KPI define those recording and tracking methods used to evaluate the effectiveness of strategies for improving performance in the organisation. SMART KPI's are *specific, measurable, attainable, relevant*, and connected to specific a *time-frame* (Klipfolio, 2019). These performance indicators—which include such measures as employee turnover rate, employee satisfaction, customer acquisition cost, and customer lifetime value—provide a measurable way of gauging improvement or regression in a company's progress toward its various goals (Jackson, August 3, 2017). If regression is indicated by these KPIs, then (according to the Washington State Department of Enterprise Services) another lean tool known as root cause analysis provides "a systematic process for identifying" the causes that lie at the root of a problem as well as suggests methods and approaches to solving these problems. (DES, 2019)...

Despite its customer-centred origins, lean philosophy also benefits the internal structure of the organisation. It goes beyond the manufacturing dimension of the organisation and penetrates to its management aspect by focusing also on the involvement of employees in its production strategies. It relies very heavily on the wide-scale integration of employees at every level of the company—from the executive boardroom to the custodial staff. Particularly through the use of *SMART KPIs* that help measure effectiveness following the free distribution of information (internal communication), lean philosophy gives employees the ability to understand the components of the organisation's goals and to gauge how well their contribution is working toward its achievement. Thus, it grants a role and voice to each person in the company and encourages each to use his/her expertise and talents to help create a unique product and a harmonious environment in which to produce it.

Founders of the lean management system identified their workforce as their most valuable asset and treated their employees accordingly. This meant not merely rewarding or compensating employees monetarily, but also granting them the creative and professional freedom necessary to exercise their strengths in the work environment. By methods geared at empowering their employees, lean management pioneers "sought to harness the power and creativity of their workers" (LMF, 2019). In light of this, it is important to recognize that many companies fail in precisely this area of corralling the expertise of all its workers and putting their talents to the best use possible. And sadly, this can be an easy mistake to make. When there is an attempt to implement lean tools, many companies claim to value their workforce while failing to demonstrate this value in the way they treat their workers.

However, lean management is about empowering all employees to feel that, as individuals, they are valuable to the organisation. This is an integral part of *compelling* employees to participate in lean—and this does not mean forcing them to participate. On the contrary, lean tools help people to feel so drawn to the purpose and objectives of the company—to feel that these objectives are so in synch with their abilities and goals—that they are drawn to the company's projects and in that way *compel themselves* to become deeply involved and committed to those goals. This leads to employee satisfaction and greater retention of workers. Let us take a more in-depth look at the lean philosophy to assess how it works in the organisational environment.

The management concepts related to lean rest on a philosophy of minimizing waste and maximizing the time and effort spent on processes that will be valuable to the company, its customers, and its employees. In production, this means focusing on the raw materials and processes that are most necessary to the manufacturing of the company's product and the elimination of all processes that fail to contribute to this. The result is that the company's revenue levels are maintained or even exceeded, while its costs are minimized—and all this without any added cost to the consumer. When transferred to processes related to human resource management, this kind of efficiency translates to the leader's interaction with employees. No effort is wasted on concerns peripheral to the wellbeing of the employee and the organisation's culture. Rather, all efforts are directed at creating an environment in which each employee feels comfortable giving their best input into the creation and execution of the organisation's goals.

The concept of an employee's best input directly corresponds to the aspect of the lean manufacturing philosophy that minimizes waste. Lean management recognizes that every employee brings a unique value to the organisation, and lean managers take responsibility to create an environment in which that employee feels valued enough to put out that best part of them for the benefit of the organisation. This is because lean philosophy ensures that the actions that benefit the organisation also benefit the employees that put them into action. For in place of an obsessive effort to control all aspects of production in the work environment, the leader committed to lean management divests some of his/her leadership responsibilities and benefits onto those employees s/he manages. The result is that each employee is encouraged to take ownership of their respective areas of contribution to the company goals; they are allowed to lead in that capacity (Kanban, 2019). Allowing employees to lead is an important part of getting them tightly integrated into their work environment.

Lean management provides a systematic way to maximise employee resources to solve work problems and positively impact the bottom line. The use of lean tools and a lean management style finds employees' strengths and puts them to good use, thereby getting the best out of all the company's resources. Thus, a company with involved employees is more likely to accrue higher revenue. Recall research cited in Chapter Six, which indicates that "a more inclusive form of ownership will be attractive to both its employees and clients, and ultimately affect the bottom line" (Wilcox, March 2, 2016). For example, when a company utilizes its human resources to their fullest potential, it saves money on unnecessary outsourcing. For when managers become fully aware of their own employees' capabilities—which might extend beyond their job descriptions—they optimize their department for producing better output at little or no additional cost. Even employees showing potential beyond their current expertise help the bottom line. Such persons might be supported by *on-the-job* training during which they continue to contribute skills they have already mastered while learning new ones. In this way, the department maximizes their capabilities and reaps (ultimately) financial benefits without much expansion to the budget. Using talents of persons already inside the department would thus save money on training new staff. The latter it is native would prove more expensive, for not only would training be necessary with respect to the particulars of the job, but new team members would also need guidance regarding the organisation's culture and workplace dynamics—both of which would require time for them to fully adjust. concerning employees more important managerial tasks inculcates a sense of ownership and encourages employees to try new and innovative ideas (Ferrier, 2019). This creative freedom supports an "innovation imperative" that has granted to companies like 3M competitive advantages in their very tough markets. It has led ultimately to such companies' ability to offer very lucrative products and services.

Lean management—the kind that grants a sense of ownership to its employees—can be implemented in any organisational situation, whether on the plant floor, in an office, in a classroom, in a warehouse, or a bank. Wherever people gather to work together toward a common goal, lean comes in to get the best out of those who work and to deliver the best to those stakeholders for whom they work—their customers, community, shareholders, or employers. Whatever the organisational situation, it is imperative that employees be allowed and *encouraged* to get involved. Anyone might ask why it is necessary to encourage employees to become a part of the lean initiative, and a significant aspect of the answer to this question is that when an employee becomes part of the solution, it gives him/her a feeling of ownership and a sense of pride concerning the company's goals.

Consider the following clear-cut ways in which the ownership afforded by lean management makes employees more valuable to the enterprise:

- Granting a level of ownership in respective aspects of production gives employees the information to do their jobs fully. This occurs because the recognition that a particular employee is an expert in a given area openly acknowledges the expertise that person has already gained. It thus encourages this newly recognized expert to make this knowledge widely available as valuable information to the others s/he will lead in the performance of projects related to that area of expertise.

- Granting ownership of designated projects gives employees control over their tasks/environment. This provides a confidence boost to them as individuals, who now believe themselves to be directing their paths within the more expansive processes of the organisation as a whole.

- Lean management's commitment to the full empowerment and optimal division of human resources reduces the uncertainty and ambiguity each employee might feel in the workplace. It does this by clearly defining each person's role according to his/her strengths and concerning the various projects being undertaken in each department. Each step along the production path is clearly understood and designated as the responsibility of some capable employee. This employee knows he is trusted because the manager makes this known by actions that not only free the employee to do his/her work but also openly recognize each of his/her tasks as a job well done.

- Lean management's tendency to grant ownership to employees expedites the process of arriving at solutions to any problems that might arise, and the speed with which this can occur minimizes the stress placed on employees—particularly those deemed responsible for outcomes, errors, etc. It also has the effect of placing more people on the task of tending to what might be wrong in the organisation or its methods. Furthermore, employee ownership of various aspects of the production process can often also splinter the blame for any problems that arise, for it allows more people to be responsible for (and move toward finding solutions to) problems or failures that might occur. The benefit of this is that employees become more willing to take risks—and risks are at the root of creative outcomes for the organisation. Thus, such ownership of various aspects of the process creates an environment in which each employee feels more secure in their position. Even though ownership means each employee manages a certain aspect of production that lays within his/her area of expertise, if each person shares—rather than takes—the credit as well as the blame, no individual will feel threatened by the possibility of failure and job loss should something go wrong. This kind of security grants the employee more confidence to go out on a limb and be creative and innovative, which translates into bigger comfort to do your job.

While lean manufacturing developed its tools around a customer-centred philosophy, lean management has appropriated these tools to strengthen the internal structure of the organisation. This management style empowers employees not only by recognizing and utilizing their strengths, but placing them in positions of leadership in their areas of expertise so that in maximizing their abilities, their input also results in a minimization of the waste of human resources that often occurs in rigidly top-down management scenarios. Thus, a sense of ownership is created in the organisation—one that grants employees incentives to become more engaged in their roles within the department and to participate with more freedom and enthusiasm in the planning and execution of strategies that benefit the company's productivity, its organisational culture, and its bottom line.

Definitions

Continuous Workflow: Ensuring that there is the fluidity with the work tasks in any given working environment.

Identifying the Value: Understanding and identifying the value of the products and/or services of any given organisation, and/or company, as well as the value that the employees bring to the products and/or services.

Value Stream: The continuous and consistent reliance and expectation and the ongoing flowing of value for the work that is produced within any given organisation.

References

Brady. (February 2012). "5S / Visual Workplace Handbook: Building the Foundation for Continuous Achievement." http://www.techni-tool.com/site/PROMO/2012-02/2012-02-Brady_5S_HandBook.pdf

DES. (2019). "Root Cause Analysis." *Risk Management.* Washington State Department of Enterprise Services. https://des.wa.gov/services/risk-management/about-risk-management/enterprise-risk-management/root-cause-analysis

Ferrier, Anthony. (2019). "Increasing Innovation and Autonomy Capability: The New Corporate Innovation Imperative." *Strategies.* innovation management.

Jackson, Ted. (August 3, 2017). "18 Key Performance Indicator

 (KPI) Examples Defined." *Clearpoint Strategy*. https://www.clearpointstrategy.com/18-key-performance-indicators/

Kanbanize. (2019). "What is Lean

 Management? Definition and

 Benefits." *Lean Management*.

 https://kanbanize.com/lean-management/what-is-lean-management/

Klipfolio. (2019). "What is a KPI? Measure

 Your Performance

 against Key Business Objectives." https://www.klipfolio.com/resources/articles/what-is-a-key-performance-indicator

Lean Manufacturing Tools (LMF). (2019).

 "What is Lean? Lean

Manufacturing Definition." *Lean Manufacturing Tools, Techniques, and Philosophy | Lean and Related Business Improvement Ideas.* http://leanmanufacturingtools.org/34/lean-manufacturing-definition-2/

Mulholland, Ben. (February 2018). "9 Lean Manufacturing Principles to Kill the Jargon and Get Quality Results." *Process St.* https://www.process.st/lean-manufacturing-principles/

Wilcox, Rachel. (March 2, 2016). "How to Make Employee Ownership Work." *Economia.* https://economia.icaew.com/features/march-2016/how-to-make-employee-ownership-work

Chapter 8: Celebrating Success

Summary:: An important aspect of cementing a company's relationship to its employees lies in how effectively it celebrates its successes and how well it constructs an ongoing mechanism for employee rejuvenation. Examples of ways to celebrate successes are noted.

Celebrations are especially important after the completion of large, and labour-intensive projects that might have contributed to employee fatigue or burn out. Celebrations and such gestures have contributed to increased engagement, motivation, and productivity among the workforce (Neely, 2019). They have also improved the internal cohesion of organisations by enhancing the corporate culture and thus establishing loyal employees. These are valuable returns for any management team, and one might think such returns might be very costly to the organisation. Yet, celebrations do not have to be elaborate or expensive; even a tiny show of gratitude or a public acknowledgment can count as a celebratory gesture and motivate or reinvigorate the employees that receive it.

How should success be defined, and should it be accorded to the individual or the group? We can begin to answer this question by first considering the benefits (if any) that the individual success has for the team. Whenever a colleague is successful in reaching a milestone or attaining a new level of competency, the improvement reflects not only a goal achieved for the company, but also an increased ability of the individual to perform his/her job functions. This means future team successes are certain. Therefore, it is beneficial for the company to celebrate individual successes. Additionally, employee celebrations give individuals a chance to share their successes and to motivate others who might be tackling similar (or even different) problems. It gives employees a chance to encourage each other and builds camaraderie among the members. Finally, celebration ties into employee recognition, which is a powerful tool for building engagement and encouraging the employee's continued efforts. While not every success can be celebrated, it is important to focus on the firsts to encourage employees to get to the next steps.

For similar reasons, it benefits a company to celebrate the successes of smaller teams within larger group settings—and on up the ladder. While it is more natural for a company to celebrate the successes of larger groups, such as departments or the organisation as a whole, often employers and managers get caught up in the routine of constantly improving output that they fail to see all how a company might be exhibiting its successes. First, one notes that an accomplishment does not have to describe an action that was completed perfectly or done exactly according to a plan/schedule (Lucas 2018). When, for example, a department (or the organisation as a whole) achieves a three percent growth in response to strategies implemented to provoke a five percent growth, a manager might consider this from the standpoint of a *failure* to meet desired goals. However, adopting a more favourable vantage will show that this reflects *improvement.* This outcome should therefore be celebrated, even as the plan is re-examined and revamped to achieve the remaining two percent. Such intermediary gains should be recognized because they allow such re-examination and provide a node at which a manager might compare achievements to baselines and benchmarks to validate the goals and the quality of the plans implemented to achieve them.

Methods and Caveats: What are some of the most effective ways to celebrate success? One important ingredient of effective celebrations is the alignment of celebratory gestures with the organisation's goals and vision. Another is the appearance of fairness: these celebrations—whether measured out to individuals or the group as a whole—should be distributed in a transparent and just manner. That is, employees should *clearly understand* which successes are being celebrated and this understanding should be coupled with a general appreciation of the reasons those persons (or successes) deserve celebrations. This way, no employee will feel left out and everyone will understand what it takes to generate these successes and celebrations. Failing to align celebratory gestures with company objectives and meting them out with fairness, celebrations will be a waste and result in a futile squandering of the organisation's efforts, resources, and opportunities for creating a better team (Mindtools).

Holding celebrations or making announcements about a team member's achievement has the potential to have both positive and negative impacts not only on the others' motivation levels but also on the confidence of the person being praised. The potential for jealousy from other employees exists; so does the potential for embarrassing the celebrated employee. So knowing *how* to recognize individuals is also important in any attempt to motivate them, and it is knowledge of one's employees that will suggest what each one will appreciate as a reward. For example, it would perhaps be unwise to celebrate the successes of an introvert by calling a great deal of attention to him/her in a large crowd. Such a prospective reward might be a *deterrent* to performance for such a person. It pays also to be sensitive to the needs of others who are not being celebrated at that moment—let the celebration be inclusive of them or at least gestured toward a future time when any of them might also be so recognized. Also, note that no matter how careful you are, some employees "can feel offended or patronized by any overt appreciation of their work as, to them, it seems to imply surprise" (MindTools, 2019). Therefore, it pays to be in touch with your team members. Being aware of your employees' personalities and the things they appreciate will be of benefit when celebrations are in order.

Do be careful, also, not to focus so much on the celebration that it loses its effect. Being fair also means being sparing in the sense that celebrations should not be performed if they are unwarranted. Remember that employees might get mixed messages if, for instance, you hold a big expensive celebration during a period in which you're trying to explain wage freezes or other cutbacks. In such a case, energy spent on celebratory efforts might appear as flattery—you trying to "butter up" employees while knowingly applying other pressures that they might find distasteful. Despite these caveats, the positive reinforcement warranted celebrations provide should always be kept in mind and pursued by the responsible and conscientious manager.

Having observed that managers should always be on the lookout for moments to celebrate, I must also emphasize that celebratory gestures do not always need to be planned out completely by the manager. It is often a very good idea to let the successful employee him-/herself share these successes with others. The successful employee often possesses the perspective and insight that it takes to solve a problem and can often provide the others with more details about the mindset necessary for success in that area. Therefore, giving that team member a platform grants the whole department a better vantage point for imagining future successes.

Research published by O. C. Tanner and company shows that almost eighty percent of employees who resign do so as a result of feeling unappreciated in their positions at work (O. C. Tanner, 2019, par. 3). Other studies have demonstrated that a statistically significant number of employees would rather be appreciated and given rewards such as greater autonomy in their positions than receive *mere* financial compensation for a job well done (Neilson and Pasternack, 2005, 29). These celebratory moments provide much of the drive that people need to continue doing their best and to accelerate the progress of the organisation. As this study by Gary L. Neilson and Bruce A. Pasternack (2005)—which was published online by Pricewaterhouse & Cooper (PWC)—shows, employees are reasonable and will contribute significantly to the organisation if they feel that successes are recognized and celebratory gestures fairly distributed:

Once people are equipped with appropriate decision rights and adequate information, motivators are what prompt them to take the actions necessary to move the organisation forward. An exhortation to follow the vision and pursue the strategy—to run faster, row harder, whatever the chosen metaphor—is only so much air if the organisation's objectives and incentives send contradictory signals (Neilson and Pasternack 2005, 29).

Naturally, these motivating gestures of celebration should be selected not merely to appease the employees, but also in a way that demonstrates alignment with the company's policies, objectives, and ethos. This point brings the discussion onto a more practical footing: that of identifying concrete methods of celebrating company, team, and individual successes.

Implementation

Some of the most obvious and overused ways of celebrating successes involve a great deal of financial expenditure on the part of the company. While these gestures—such as bonuses, raises, and promotions—have their place, other methods of celebrating success exist that present a manager's message of appreciation to employees just as effectively. Innovative companies and their leaders have learned that team lunches, dinners, a corporate (or team) day off, team building activities—even birthday parties and lunches/coffee dates with the boss—can be effective ways of recognizing successes. In fact, in many cases, a simple verbal "thank you" also sends a strong message to the employee about his/her recent creditable performance. However, let's take a closer look at some of these gestures.

Team lunches, dinners, and parties are good ways to celebrate the success of a single person or the whole team in a group setting. The gesture sends a simultaneous message to everyone that the manager notices and appreciates the efforts of the team and is willing to expend time and resources in supporting those efforts. Such public celebrations can boost the confidence of an individual as well. If the office or team is small enough that birthday parties are the norm, the manager might use such opportunities to highlight that member's successes throughout the past year. This means keeping accurate records of individual successes, and it sends a strong message to the employee (and the team) that their large and small efforts are remembered and important.

Team building activities and days off can be combined or kept separate. However, both strengthen the cohesion of the group and can imbue a stressed-out workforce with the relaxation and rejuvenation required to continue moving towards the organisation's objectives. Day-off activities can be chosen by the team itself via a poll, and these may take the form of a film screening, a day at the park, an outing to watch a live baseball game, or some other fun activity that engages everyone and gives them some breathing room away from the office. Along similar lines, team activities must be chosen carefully in order not to increase the stress of the group: select activities that are interesting and engaging but do not put employees on the spot or make them feel awkward. However, once you have selected a winning group of activities that your team appreciates, utilize them wisely to increase their morale, relieve their stress, and celebrate their successes.

One-on-one activities can also make team members feel special and demonstrate the manager's appreciation for recent success. Having lunch or coffee with the boss takes the individual employee out of the office and places him/her in a privileged position that draws positive attention to success. It is important to recognize during this moment of individual attention that a scenario such as "lunch with the boss" might be a stressful one for the employee. So, in order not to defeat the purpose of the gesture, do and say things during these occasions, that make that employee comfortable.

An organisation can cement its relationship with its employees by consistently and fairly celebrating the successes of each and/or of the group. When management considers the benefits of the individual as a benefit to the whole group and celebrates accordingly, that gesture motivates the individual to continue along that path and urges the group to follow suit. The result is that a greater proportion of the workforce starts putting out more effort toward the company's growth. Similarly, a celebration of smaller team successes, have a comparable effect. Yet these positive results can be better achieved when the company aligns its celebrations with its general goals, visions, and ethos. A company's integration of its celebrations with its corporate identity and standards will cause it to reap higher benefits and truly come to embody the adage that positive reinforcement begets the desired behaviours—ones that lead to further individual successes and overall corporate growth.

Definition

Celebrations: Ensuring that the celebrations and the successes of an organisation are paramount to improving employee engagement, having moments to "stop and to smell the roses" of success of an organisation, and to support continued improvement in workplace professional relationships.

References

Lucas, Susan. (2019). "How to Celebrate Success at Work: Tips about How to Celebrate Success as an Individual and as a Team." *Balance Careers.* https://www.thebalancecareers.com/how-to-celebrate-success-at-work-4160403

MindTools. (2019). "Celebrating Achievement: How to Make Your Team Feels Good." *MindTools: Essential Skills for an Excellent Career.* https://www.mindtools.com/pages/article/celebrating-achievement.htm

Neely, Sydney. (2019). "Does Celebrating Accomplishments in the Workplace Promote Future Success?" *Chron.* https://work.chron.com/celebrating-accomplishments-workplace-promote-future-success-20748.html

Neilson, Gary L., and Bruce A. Pasternack. (2005). *Results: keep what's good, fix what's wrong, and unlock great performance.* Crown Business, 2005. https://www.strategyand.pwc.com/media/file/Strategyand-Results-Book-Except.pdf

O. C. Tanner. (2019). "Appreciation Changes Everything." https://www.octanner.com/insights/infographics/appreciation-changes-everything.html

Conclusion

Granting Joy: An employee engagement roadmap is a book that will help team leaders, managers, and supervisors to be better at the jobs, stronger with their career path, plus helping employees to learn how to love their jobs, and to make the best out of each moment they are at work.

With the common-sense driven roadmap for engaging employees, I have been able to build my leadership style that has worked, and continues to work, for me in my career. Again, it is a product of 20+ years of experience working in healthy environments, observing and learning from thoughtful leaders, my training in and out of academia, and personal reflection. Of course, it all hasn't been rosy — we all should learn from the negative experiences too; but by adopting the ideas shared in this book, I aim to help you see, in short, that running an operation with engaged employees can release the workforce's potential and is well proven to deliver bottom-line results.

Driving employee engagement is a leader's function but in my opinion, each employee plays a role in his/her engagement. Just like communication, engaged employees stem from top-down and bottom-up efforts — everyone's positive attitude contributes.

This roadmap is not a quick fix, it is, however, a guide to develop your leadership style in a fashion that today's employees will appreciate and gravitate towards, enabling your success and the success of your team and business.

Take this schematic of the roadmap and use it to drive your leadership style that engages employees, enabling overall business, people, and career successes.

Common-Sense Driven Plan Roadmap – At the Centre is Employee Engagement

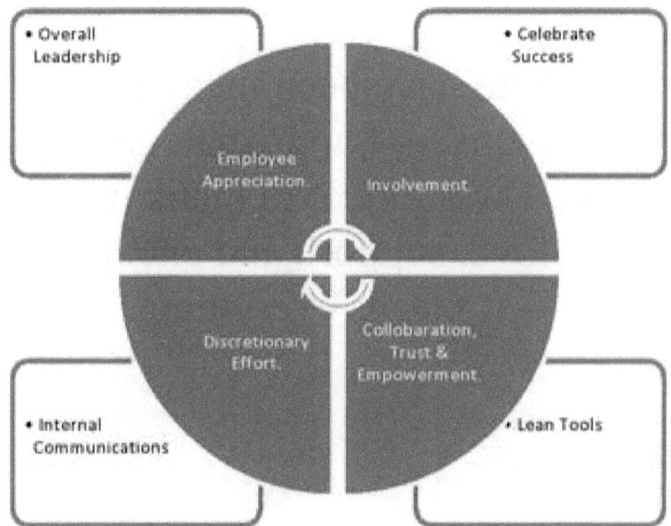

Acknowledgments

In my life, there have been many teachers and many lessons — I appreciate them all. Most of all, I would like to thank my parents for all their love, support, and encouragement — it means everything.

About the Author

Joy Grant is a professional engineer with an MBA and Lean Six Sigma Black Belt. Grant writes this book delivering a vital perspective that can hone the leadership style of today's team leader. And, this book provides a proven and practical roadmap that can help you to engage your team and improve the work environment, wherever you may work.

With more than twenty years of experience, Grant is finally sharing what has worked for her and other leaders in the various Fortune 500 companies where she has been successfully employed. Use this book in your employee engagement journey, ***Granting Joy: An employee engagement roadmap***.

www.ingramcontent.com/pod-product-compliance
Lightning Source LLC
Chambersburg PA
CBHW031945170526
45157CB00002B/392